Success Through Teamwork

A Practical Guide To Interpersonal Team Dynamics

Richard Y. Chang

Richard Chang Associates, Inc.
Publications Division
Irvine, California

Success Through Teamwork

A Practical Guide To Interpersonal Team Dynamics

Richard Y. Chang

Library of Congress Catalog Card Number
93-74770

ISBN 1-883553-25-3

Third printing April 1996

Richard Chang Associates, Inc.
Publications Division
41 Corporate Park, Suite 230
Irvine, CA 92714
(800) 756-8096 • Fax (714) 756-0853

ACKNOWLEDGMENTS

About The Author

Richard Y. Chang is President and CEO of Richard Chang Associates, Inc., a diversified organizational improvement consulting firm based in Irvine, California. He is internationally recognized for his management strategy, quality improvement, organization development, customer satisfaction, and human resource development expertise.

The author would like to acknowledge the support of the entire team of professionals at Richard Chang Associates, Inc. for their contribution to the guidebook development process. In addition, special thanks are extended to the many client organizations who have helped us shape the practical ideas and proven methods shared in this guidebook.

Additional Credits

Editors: Candyce Norvell and Sarah Ortlieb Fraser

Reviewers: Anthony Harris, Ruth Stingley and Pamela Wade

Graphic Layout: Suzanne Jamieson, Doug Westfall and Jacqueline Westfall

Cover Design: John Odam Design Associates

PREFACE

The 1990's have already presented individuals and organizations with some very difficult challenges to face and overcome. So who will have the advantage as we move toward the year 2000 and beyond?

The advantage will belong to those with a commitment to continuous learning. Whether on an individual basis or as an entire organization, one key ingredient to building a continuous learning environment is *The Practical Guidebook Collection* brought to you by the Publications Division of Richard Chang Associates, Inc.

After understanding the future *"learning needs"* expressed by our clients and other potential customers, we are pleased to publish *The Practical Guidebook Collection*. These guidebooks are designed to provide you with proven, *"real-world"* tips, tools, and techniques on a wide range of subjects that you can apply in the workplace and/or on a personal level immediately!

Once you've had a chance to benefit from *The Practical Guidebook Collection*, please feel free to share your feedback with us. Your feedback is so important that we've included a brief *Evaluation and Feedback Form* at the end of the guidebook that you may fax to us at (714) 756-0853.

With your feedback, we can continuously improve the resources we are providing through the Publications Division of Richard Chang Associates, Inc.

Wishing you successful reading,

Richard Y. Chang
President and CEO
Richard Chang Associates, Inc.

TABLE OF CONTENTS

"The achievements of an organization are the results of the combined efforts of each individual."

Vince Lombardi, football coach

"Team spirit is what gives so many companies an edge over their competitors."

George Clements

CHAPTER ONE

INTRODUCTION

The success of any team depends on the individuals who make up the team. That's no secret. If team members don't communicate effectively, are in continual conflict, and lack motivation, the team will not succeed.

However, if you teach the members communication skills, train them to resolve conflict, and motivate them to excel, the team can succeed. You'll feel the positive energy. And you'll see results that only an effective team can achieve.

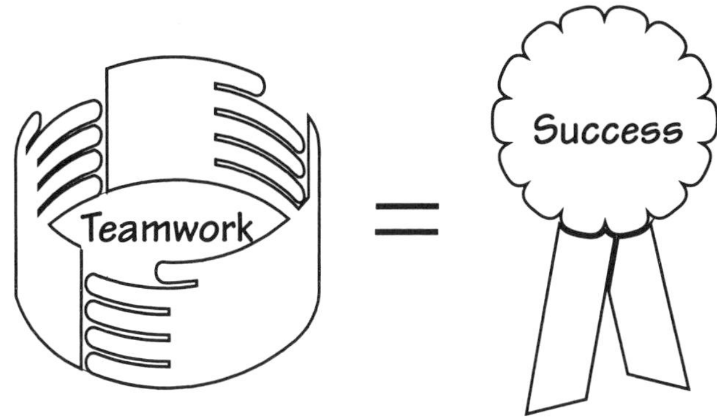

Why Read This Guidebook?

If you're already using effective teamwork techniques, you don't need this book. Then again, you wouldn't have picked it up unless your team needed improvement. You can use this guidebook's techniques to improve your team's performance.

This guidebook outlines ways to help your team work together better. It will take some of the frustration out of group communication and conflict, and help you increase motivation and commitment. It will allow you to devote your time and energy to what's important—reaching your team's goals.

Who Should Read This Guidebook?

Are you a member of a team that's having trouble communicating? Does your team seem too diverse to work together effectively? Perhaps you're part of a team that gets along great, but gets nothing done. Maybe you're a new team leader, and your goal is to sidestep the problems many teams experience.

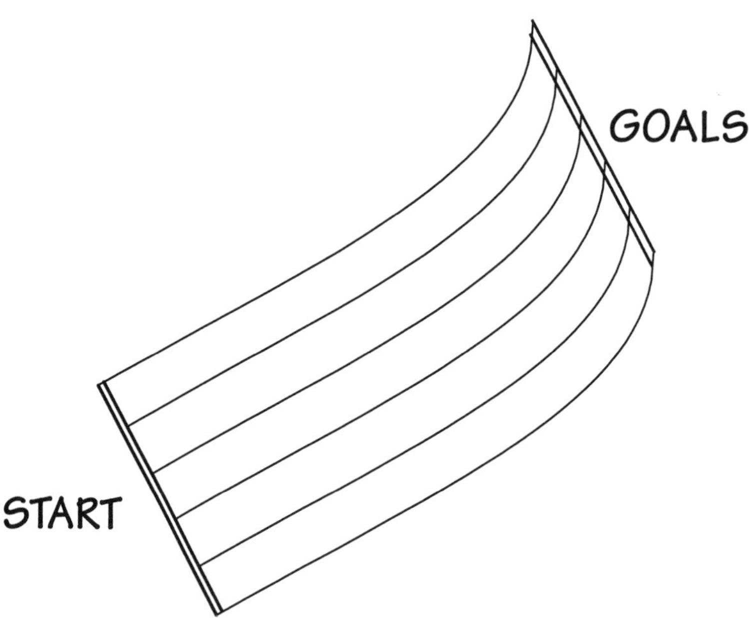

Whether your team has just formed or has been meeting for years, if you want to improve your team's performance, read this guidebook. You don't have to be a team leader—motivated team members can do much to change a team's dynamics.

If you want to move your team from apathetic to energetic, from conflict-ridden to solution-oriented, or from mediocre to motivated, this guidebook is for you. It will show you that all teams can learn to be top performers.

When And How To Use It

Use this guidebook as a resource when starting a team or to improve dynamics in a group that's been working together for some time. Distribute it to individual team members as a guide and discuss it during team meetings. Alternatively, use it to address specific issues as the need arises.

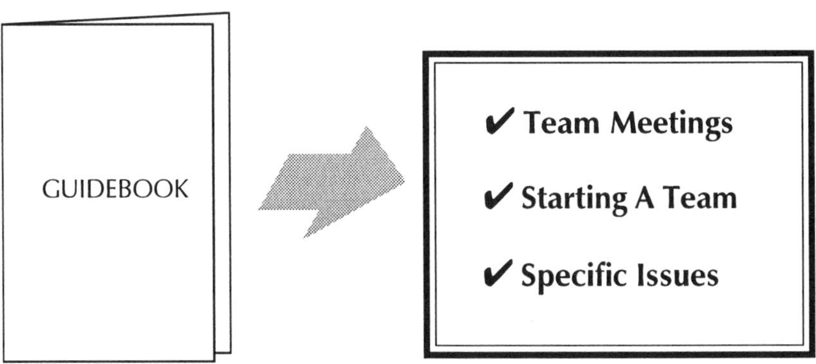

No matter how you use this guidebook, the more you use it, the more likely you are to develop a successful team. And that's a goal worth reaching for!

CHAPTER TWO

Improving Team Dynamics

Whether your team is a committee, a task force, or a project group, you'll need to work together efficiently and effectively to reach your goals. But many obstacles can stall your progress. Differing attitudes, ineffective communication, and lack of motivation can create chaos in a team.

Simply identifying team members and goals isn't enough. You can't lump a group of people together, tell them what you want them to accomplish, and expect everything to run smoothly. You'll encounter many obstacles along the way.

However, if you understand team dynamics and use techniques to improve your team's effectiveness, you'll reach your goals. And this guidebook will help you do it.

The Keys To Effective Teamwork

Teams are people. And people have certain needs when working together in teams. These include: effective communication, active listening, successfully resolving the conflicts that inevitably arise when people work in groups, understanding and adapting to the diverse backgrounds of other team members, and last, but not least, maintaining a sense of motivation among all team members.

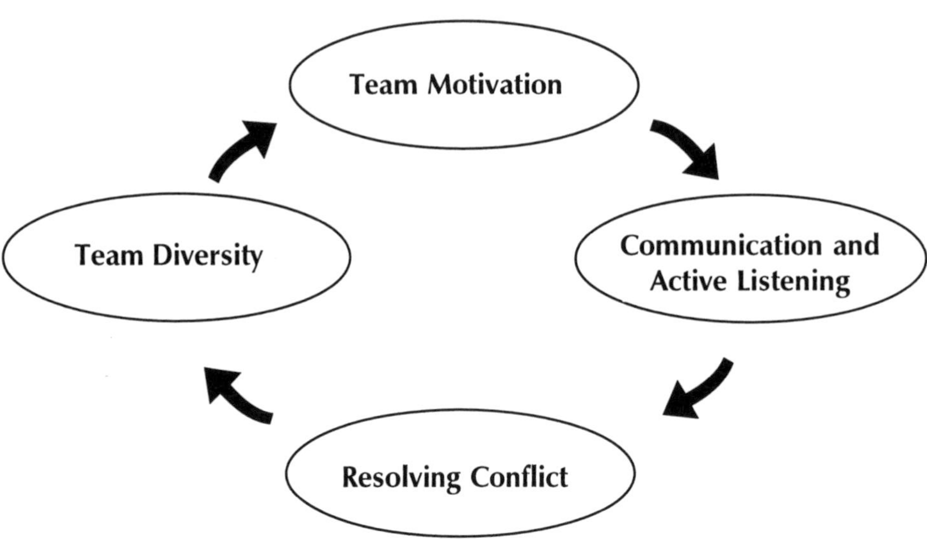

This is not a complete list of all the factors that affect the interpersonal dynamics among team members. However, by focusing on these key areas, your team will be well on its way to reaping all the benefits of true teamwork.

Communication

Communication is the essence of successful teamwork. Effective communication is the starting point for understanding, interpretation, and action. On the other hand, ineffective team communication can lead to misunderstanding, misinterpretation, and either inaction or inappropriate action.

Chapter Three covers the elements of effective communication, and points out barriers and enhancers to improved team communication. Put these ideas to work to enhance interactions within your team and with others in your organization.

Active listening

Effective team communication involves two sets of responsibilities: that of the sender of the message, and that of the receiver. Techniques such as paraphrasing, reflecting the implications of the message, inviting contributions, and reflecting the underlying feelings, are covered in Chapter Four.

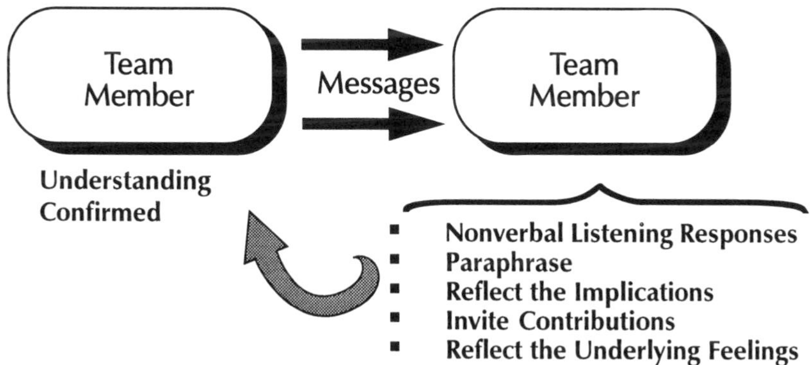

These techniques contribute to closing the communication loop, ensuring that team members not only *"hear"* each other, but confirm their understanding, and as a result, take the appropriate actions.

Resolving conflict

Team members often have their own individual and instinctual approach to dealing with conflict. Some avoid it, some confront it objectively, and others may let emotions drive their reactions. When members of the same team are using a mix of these approaches, the results can be counterproductive, often making the situation worse instead of resolving it. The solution—have team members use an effective, consistent approach.

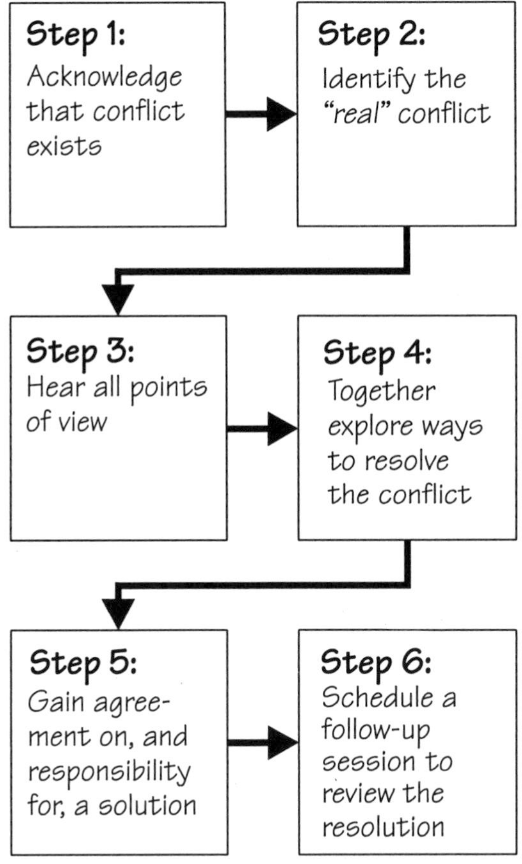

Chapter Five presents a six-step model your team can use to ensure a consistent approach to resolving conflicts.

Team diversity

The diversity of the backgrounds of your team members can present both challenges and opportunities. Challenges arise when team members misinterpret each other's messages or actions, or respond in unintended ways.

This same diversity presents opportunities for teams to draw on each person's strengths and uniquenesses to learn from each other. Team members have to recognize their uniquenesses for what they are, adapt accordingly, and capitalize on what they cannot change.

Chapter Six describes how your team can use certain processes to take full advantage of team member diversity.

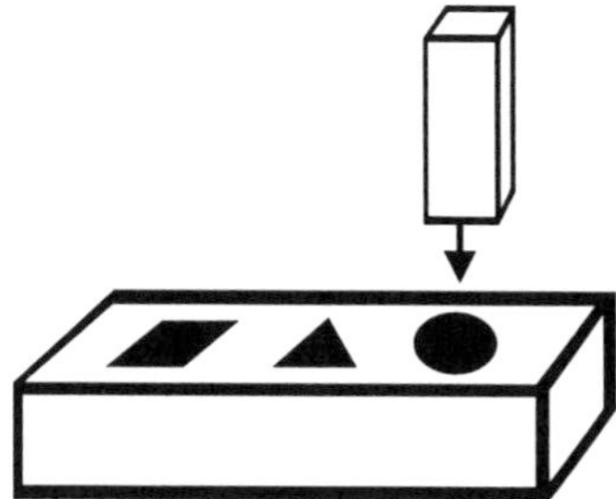

Team motivation

Motivation is the spark plug of team performance—it inspires commitment, innovation, and teamwork. But motivation can't be taken for granted. Team leaders and members need to be aware of the factors affecting motivation and techniques they can use to enhance and maintain motivation levels.

Chapter Seven presents techniques your team can use to focus on team member motivation on an ongoing basis.

Chapter Two Worksheet: Your Team's Effectiveness

1. a.) What instances of *ineffective* team communication have you experienced or observed lately?

b.) What were the causes of the ineffective communication?

c.) What were the consequences?

2. a.) What instances of *effective* communication have you experienced or observed lately?

b.) What contributed to the effectiveness?

3. Which active listening techniques do your team members use most?

4. What are the most common causes of conflict on your team?

5. What role has the diversity of team member backgrounds played in your team's successes and challenges?

6. What challenges has your team had to deal with in terms of maintaining its motivation?

TUNING IN TO COMMUNICATION CUES

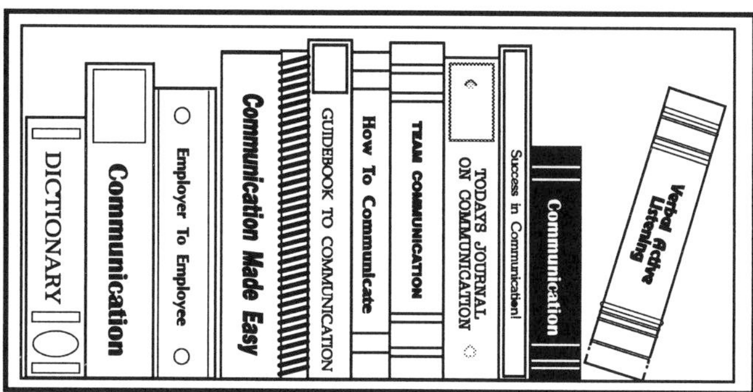

Communication is critical to your team's success. If your group members communicate well, your chance of success improves. But good communication is difficult. Have you ever noticed the large number of books published on this topic? If communication was simple, bookstores wouldn't stock their shelves with how-to's on the subject.

In an organizational setting, the term *"communication"* may have different meaning for different people, depending on their perspectives. And often, their perspectives are negative. Some common issues that have come up in hundreds of organizational surveys include:

- Employees feel there is not enough communication from management.
- Department members feel that other department members use communication *(or lack thereof)* to *"protect their turfs."*
- Individuals feel they are good at communicating, while others are not.

In this chapter we will focus on communication as an individual and team issue, where improvement will lead to results for the whole organization.

What Is Effective Communication?

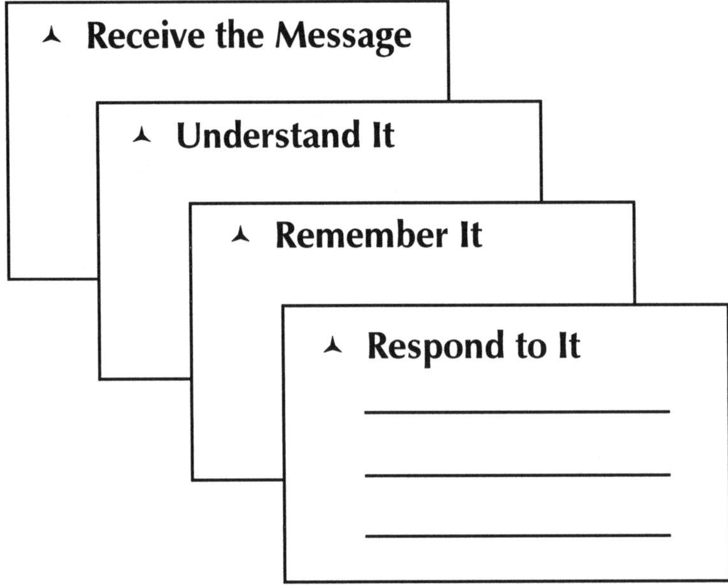

Communication is effective only when the people to whom you're communicating receive your message, understand it, remember it, and—here's the clincher—respond to it appropriately. If your message doesn't succeed in these four areas, you're not communicating.

A team that doesn't communicate experiences division and lack of commitment. It wastes time and accomplishes little. Discussions drag on with little or no progress. However, a team that communicates well makes timely progress and achieves its goals.

For example, take these two teams . . .

from the same organization, PFI Pharmaceuticals:

Team A: ***PFI formed a project group . . .***

from its accounting department to plan a budget for the upcoming year. Maria, a senior financial officer and leader of the team, explained the group's goals and asked for input on how to achieve them. She gave all members an opportunity to contribute and listened carefully to their concerns. Before the end of the first meeting, Maria asked the group to restate its goals and made sure that all members knew what tasks they had to complete before the next meeting.

Team B: ***The other team was a task force . . .***

composed of individuals from various departments—marketing, accounting, public relations, and customer service. This task force had to address a lawsuit filed against the organization over drug side effects.

Sam, a legal representative for PFI, headed the first meeting and distributed a long list of questions that he needed answered. Without consulting other team members, Sam divided the questions among them and asked that they return with detailed answers at the next meeting.

The task force members were unhappy, since most had to answer questions outside their areas of expertise. For example, Brenda, the public relations manager, was to research shipping records to find out when and where the company had shipped the drug. Marcus, a marketing representative, was to find out whether the company had sent recall notices. After the meeting, the team members grumbled about receiving inappropriate tasks. At the next meeting, a disgruntled team assembled, and few members had completed their tasks. . . .

Differences in the team leaders' communication led to differences in the performance of the two teams. In Team B's interaction, even though the task force members received, understood, and remembered the message, they did not respond the way Sam wanted. Maria, on the other hand, had made the communication with her team a two-way process, asking for and listening to their input.

What Works Best?

The type of communication that works best is everyday, face-to-face dialogue. Although it may come as a surprise, it's certainly not an innovative technique. Let's look at how a common situation was handled in two different ways:

> Your team leader sends a memo to remind you about tomorrow's meeting and to ask for your input on a specific topic. Alternatively, your team leader speaks to you personally and says: *"Don't forget our meeting tomorrow at 3 P.M. And, hey, I'd really appreciate it if you'd come prepared with some ideas about our topic. We could use your expertise. I'm glad you're part of the team."*

Which method would have more impact on you? There's no doubt that face-to-face dialogue is more effective.

Just think how the first meeting . . .
of PFI's task force could have been different if Sam had used face-to-face dialogue. Brenda and Marcus would have been able to express their doubts about how Sam delegated the questions. Instead, Sam cut corners, thus cutting the effectiveness of his communication. . . .

Unfortunately, knowing the type of communication that works best won't solve all communication problems. You also need to master active listening, peer feedback, and conflict resolution, which the following chapters cover. You need to tune in to nonverbal communication, use the communication process to your advantage, and be aware of the communication environment.

Tips For Good Communication

The following tips will help your team use the communication process to its advantage. Notice how differently effective and ineffective communicators respond.

TIPS FOR GOOD COMMUNICATION		
TIPS	**THE INEFFECTIVE COMMUNICATOR**	**THE EFFECTIVE COMMUNICATOR**
Find areas of interest	Tunes out dry subject	Seeks opportunities; asks, *"What's in it for me?"*
Judge content, not delivery	Tunes out if delivery is poor	Judges content; skips over delivery errors
Hold your fire	Tends to interrupt or argue	Withholds judgment until comprehension is complete
Work at listening	Shows no energy output; attention is *"faked"*	Works hard; exhibits active body state
Resist distractions	Distracted easily	Fights or avoids distractions; tolerates bad habits; knows how to concentrate

TIPS FOR GOOD COMMUNICATION (CONT'D)		
Tips	**The Ineffective Communicator**	**The Effective Communicator**
Exercise your mind	Resists difficult material; seeks light, recreational material	Uses heavier material as an exercise for the mind
Keep your mind open	Reacts to emotional words	Interprets "*colorful*" words—*does not* get hung up on them
Capitalize on the fact that thought is faster than speech	Tends to daydream with slow speakers	Mentally sums up; weighs evidence; challenges; listens "*between the lines*"

Use these tactics daily. If you focus on a different one each day or week, you'll find your communication becoming more effective. The more you practice, the easier it becomes. The results—improved team dynamics—will speak for themselves.

Note: This table also appears in the Appendix as a *"Reproducible Form"* for you to copy and use in discussing these tips with your team members.

Understanding Nonverbal Cues

Most communication is not verbal! Even when you aren't speaking, you are still communicating nonverbally.

In the communication process, you affect other team members and they affect you without saying a word. You send positive and negative messages by the way you communicate nonverbally. The following table contains several nonverbal actions and their perceived meanings.

Nonverbal Response	What It May Indicate
Bouncing your leg	✓ Impatience ✓ Urgency ✓ Lack of interest
Raising an eyebrow	✓ Disbelief ✓ Questioning ✓ Surprise
Nodding your head	✓ Approval ✓ Encouragement ✓ Understanding
Leaning forward	✓ Interest ✓ Concentration ✓ Care
Remaining silent	✓ Concentration ✓ Interest ✓ Respect

NONVERBAL RESPONSE	WHAT IT MAY INDICATE (CONTINUED)
Frowning	✓ Disapproval ✓ Sadness ✓ Lack of understanding
Looking away	✓ Distraction ✓ Impatience ✓ Lack of interest
Rolling your eyes	✓ Disapproval ✓ Disbelief ✓ Lack of understanding
Restlessness	✓ Lack of interest ✓ Message too lengthy ✓ Discomfort

In a team or small group, you have many opportunities to send or respond to nonverbal messages. For example, if your team members are giving you nonverbal cues that they don't understand or accept your message, you can respond by clarifying it or by changing your approach.

Maria, the leader of PFI's budget team . . .

presented the team's goals and the dates she expected to meet those goals. Bob and Tina, two of Maria's colleagues, began sending nonverbal signs of disapproval: Bob began frowning, and Tina leaned back in her chair and folded her arms. Maria stopped in mid-sentence. *"Bob and Tina,"* she said, *"I sense that you're having some difficulty with what I'm saying. Can I clarify anything for you?"*

"You're right," Bob said. *"I don't see how we can accomplish everything when you want us to. We're already overloaded with work."* Tina nodded.*"That's a very good point,"* Maria responded. *"How do the rest of you feel about this issue?"*

By observing nonverbal cues, Maria was able to communicate effectively with her team. Had she ignored or not been aware of those cues, she would have lost ground with the team. Instead she capitalized on an opportunity to communicate care and concern.

Chapter Three Worksheet: Improving Communication

1. Think about the barriers/enhancers to communication and list examples of those that have caused problems in your team or have enhanced your communication.

a) Noise

b) Channel

c) Sender/Receiver frame of reference

d) Feedback

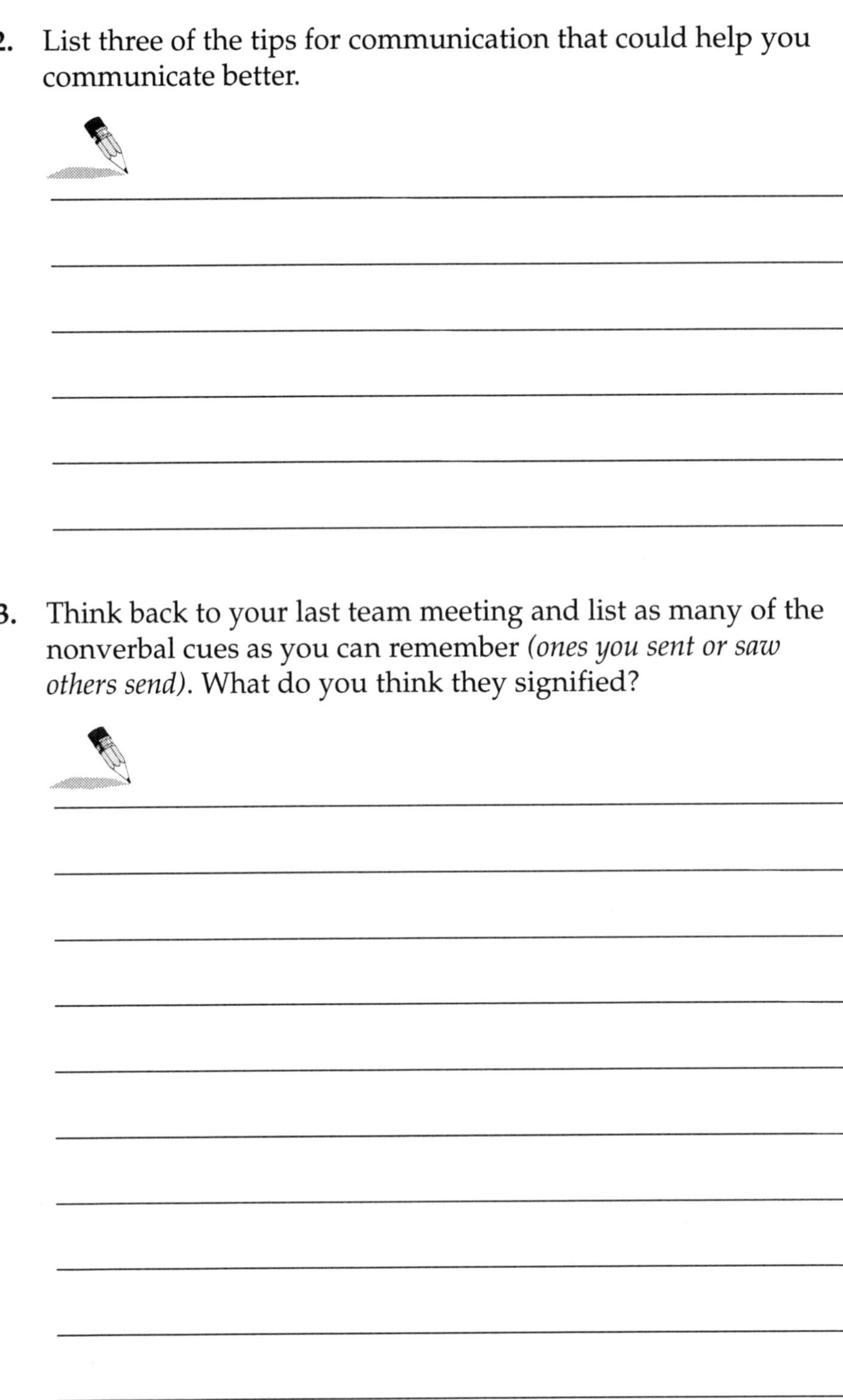

2. List three of the tips for communication that could help you communicate better.

3. Think back to your last team meeting and list as many of the nonverbal cues as you can remember *(ones you sent or saw others send)*. What do you think they signified?

4. How can your team change or act on tips from question # 2?

USING ACTIVE LISTENING SKILLS

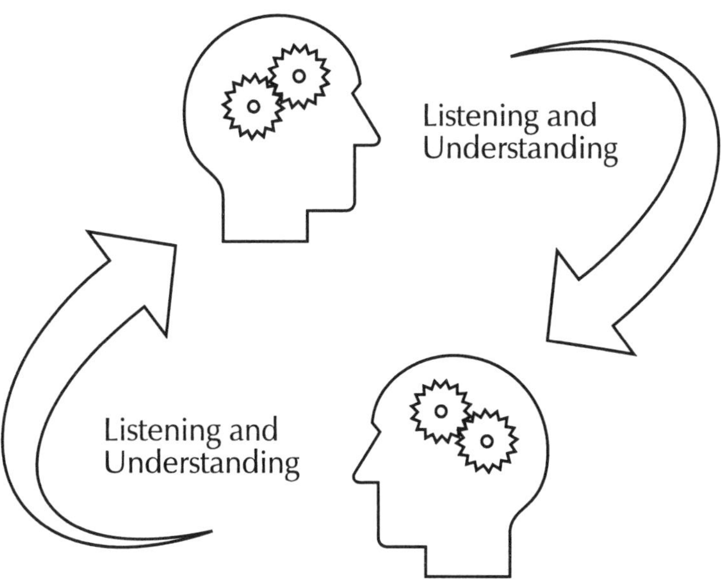

Communication is a two-way process. If you aren't listening, and understanding what someone else is saying, there's no communication.

In any team, active listening is absolutely critical. Most of us focus on our responsibilities and actions as senders, and forget our responsibilities as receivers. We often think of listening as passive. But it's not. Active listening is a skill that can keep communication moving forward.

Active Listening Techniques

Active listening techniques help you communicate to others that you have heard and understood them. Implementing the following five active listening techniques can help your team communicate more effectively.

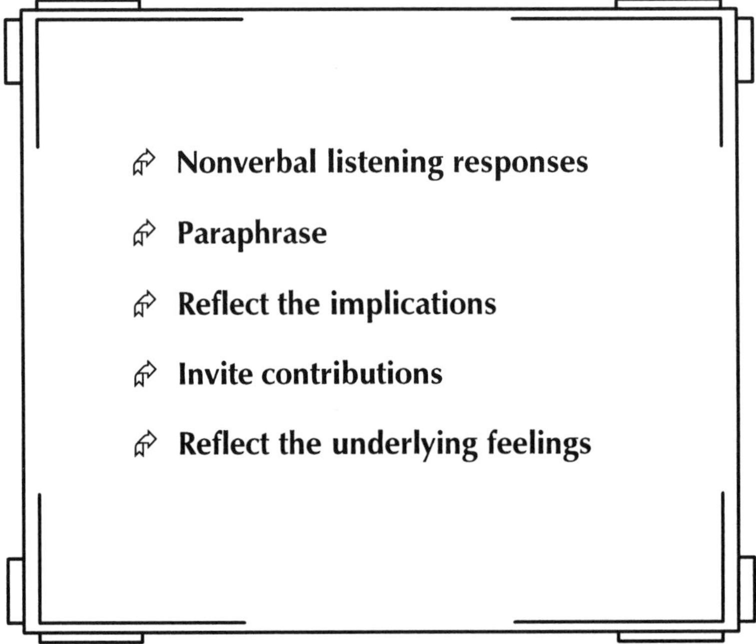

Let's look at each of them in turn, examining examples of the techniques, their advantages, and tips for their use.

Nonverbal listening responses

Used in conjunction with verbal active listening techniques, nonverbal responses increase your communication power.

Beware, however, of using these nonverbal cues without really listening to what another person is saying. Such *"fake listening"* won't help you, and may even hurt you in the long run if another team member discovers that you weren't listening.

EXAMPLES	ADVANTAGES	TIPS FOR USE
✔Looking into the speaker's eyes ✔Nodding approvingly ✔Leaning toward the speaker	✔Communicates message and personal acceptance ✔Shows understanding and interest	✔Be sincere ✔Be consistent ✔Resist external distractions

That's what happened to Jim, . . .

an insurance claims representative and a member of a team formed to increase productivity in the claims department. Jim's mind was elsewhere when Sue, the team's leader, discussed a new procedure they were to implement. Later in the week, Sue called Jim. She was irritated because he was not using the new procedure. *"I thought you understood it,"* she said. *"You were listening carefully in the meeting, and when I asked if you understood, you nodded."* . . .

Don't fall into the trap Jim did. Use nonverbal responses to help you focus on speakers, not as a camouflage to tune them out.

Paraphrase

Paraphrasing is an active listening technique that helps you understand exactly what the other person is saying, and identifies you as a careful listener. Use it regularly, and you'll avoid having to later clarify points you thought you understood at the time.

EXAMPLES	ADVANTAGES	TIPS FOR USE
✔"As I understand it . . ." ✔"What you're saying is . . ." ✔"If I could summarize . . ."	✔Shows that you are listening intently to the message ✔Clarifies the sender's "true" message ✔Helps you to truly understand the message	✔Listen intently ✔Paraphrase fairly often ✔May interrupt to do so

If Jim had made a habit . . .

of paraphrasing, he wouldn't have been in *"hot water"* with Sue. He would have realized at the time that he hadn't been listening well enough to be able to paraphrase what she'd said about the new procedure. He could have asked Sue to explain it again, and implemented it along with the rest of the team. . . .

Reflect the implications

When you reflect the implications of a message, you're going beyond merely understanding the words themselves. You're thinking ahead, reading between the lines, and showing that communication is a two-way channel.

EXAMPLES	ADVANTAGES	TIPS FOR USE
✔"Would that mean that . . ." ✔"Are you saying that . . ." ✔"Would that help with . . ."	✔Communicates "genuine" interest in the message ✔Exhibits understanding of the message or issue being communicated	✔Allow the speaker to be in control ✔Avoid trying to persuade ✔Avoid "one-upmanship"

The danger in this technique is that you may come across as superior or overly aggressive if your interpretation of the message is incorrect. Your purpose is to show genuine interest. Nonverbal responses are especially helpful in this instance. Show your deference to the speaker while communicating interest and understanding, and you'll bypass the danger.

Sue's team was trying to revamp . . .

the insurance claims process. Policyholders sent claims for prescription drugs and doctors' services to the same address, and the mailroom had to sort them before sending them to the two departments. As a result, claims took weeks to process, and many prescription drug users needed to purchase another prescription before the company reimbursed them for their previous ones.

Matthew, one of the team members, made a suggestion. *"What if people sending claims included the department number on the addressed envelope?"* Sue paused a moment and moved toward Matthew. *"Now, there's a thought,"* she said. *"Are you saying that would make it easier for the mailroom to sort the claims? That they wouldn't have to open the letters to forward them?"* Matthew nodded. By listening actively and reflecting implications, Sue communicated interest in Matthew's suggestion and revealed that she understood it. . . .

Invite contributions

Inviting contributions, another active listening technique, allows you to show interest and to follow-up on a good thought. It can encourage a shy speaker to continue explaining an idea, or communicate openness when you don't necessarily agree with the speaker.

EXAMPLES	ADVANTAGES	TIPS FOR USE
✔"What happened then?" ✔"Can you give me an example?" ✔"Tell me more about . . ."	✔Communicates a desire to hear more about the topic ✔Allows time for the sender and receiver to understand the message ✔Promotes openness	✔Should not be used exclusively ✔Should follow paraphrasing and reflecting ✔Avoid "over-exposing" the speaker

Sue and Matthew had just begun discussing . . .

Matthew's idea when Dianne, another team member, piped up, *"It's not going to work!"* Matthew turned his attention toward Dianne. *"I hear you saying that it's not an effective idea,"* he began. *"Can you tell me why you think that?"*

Matthew could have begun arguing with Dianne. Instead, he used active listening to keep the communication effective. Active listening encourages everybody to keep an open mind. . . .

Reflect the underlying feelings

Reflecting the underlying feelings is especially effective when the content of a message is emotional. It shows that you're a sensitive listener, able to put yourself in someone else's shoes.

EXAMPLES	ADVANTAGES	TIPS FOR USE
✔"If that happened to me, I'd be upset . . ." ✔"How did that make you feel?" ✔"I suppose that must make you annoyed." ✔"That must have been satisfying."	✔Communicates a "genuine" understanding of the message and its implications ✔Helps the receiver in empathizing with the sender	✔Avoid telling the speaker how they "ought" to feel ✔Avoid pressing for information ✔Avoid evaluating the speaker

Let's jump back to when Sue confronted Jim . . .

about not using the new procedure. Sue knew that Jim had not listened and she had expressed her disapproval. But watch how Jim uses active listening this time:

"I can tell that you're annoyed with me," Jim says. *"You're darn right I am,"* Sue responds. *"Well, Sue,"* Jim begins, *"I'd be angry too, if I were in your shoes. I'm sorry that I appeared to be listening when I wasn't. Perhaps you could explain the procedure to me again on the condition that I promise to give you my full attention. "*. . .

When you listen with empathy to the feelings and ideas of others, they feel genuinely understood.

Benefits Of Active Listening

Every team member needs to master the skill of active listening. Practice active listening until it becomes second nature. Active listening offers these advantages:

- Lets team members vent; gives them what they may want: an ear!
- Lets team members feel appreciated, understood, and accepted
- Develops competence; enhances members' ability to identify problems and solutions; improves reasoning and judgment
- Lets team members remain responsible and accountable; keeps the "*monkey*" on their backs and therefore lightens your workload
- Avoids the "*Yes, but . . .*" trap
- Allows members to think for themselves; builds independence
- Saves time for all involved
- Removes loaded or negative language by paraphrasing
- Results in a better working relationship

Active listening benefits both speakers and listeners. If every member of your team uses active listening, you'll reap a double reward!

Chapter Four Worksheet: Working On Active Listening

1. The following two on-the-job situations could occur anywhere. Read each case as if you were listening, then (1) identify the best one or two active listening techniques, and (2) describe how you would respond *(write the actual words you would use).*

a) Marie, a supervisor on your team who is conscientious and usually quiet, has lost her patience. She is responding irritably to routine changes, decisions, and problems, and has become difficult to work with. You are talking to her after a meeting when she says to you:

"Let's face it—sometimes we have no control and get no respect or recognition around here. Basically, we're glorified laborers. People change our objectives and priorities constantly without thinking through the impacts of the changes. For example, now I have to attend four hours of training classes a week, and do another four hours of assignments. How am I supposed to get all that done and increase my production, too?!"

❒ Which active listening technique(s) would you use?

____

____

____

____

____

____

____

❐ How would you respond *(i.e., in your exact words)*?

b) One of your work group members, Dan, is outspoken, fault-finding, and demanding. He used to be a *"team player,"* but with recent organizational and staff changes, he is becoming an obstacle to progress. His staff is avoiding him as much as possible. Dan says to you:

"The people who work around here are just plain lazy and unfriendly. I tell them what they ought to do, but they don't listen to me. I'm getting tired of repeating myself and having to follow-up on things that they should be doing!"

❐ Which active listening technique(s) would you use?

❐ How would you respond *(i.e., in your exact words)*?

2. Think back to a recent interaction with one of your team members that would have benefited from active listening.

   a) Which active listening technique(s) would have been appropriate?

   b) How would you respond if this situation were to happen again?

RESOLVING CONFLICTS

In any team that's really working toward its goals, there's bound to be conflict. Differences will occur. But the outcome doesn't have to be negative. Conflict can provide opportunities to create new solutions. The key is how team members respond to conflicts.

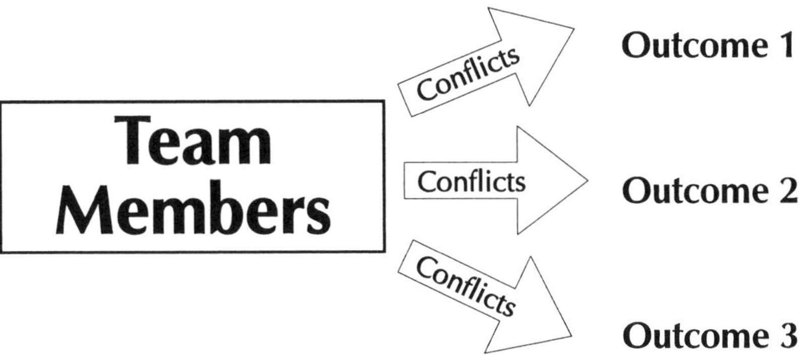

It's vital for team members to understand that conflict or disagreement is inevitable and not inherently good or bad.

Conflict can destroy your team's progress if left unmanaged; it can lead to sound decision making if managed well. The outcome of conflict depends on how you and your team manage it.

Cues To Conflict

You may get so involved in a team's discussion that you fail to notice a conflict between members. Following are some cues to help you recognize conflict:

- Team members make comments and suggestions with much emotion.
- Team members attack others' ideas before they are finished expressing them.
- Team members accuse one another of not understanding the real point.
- Team members take sides and refuse to compromise.
- Team members attack one another on a personal level in subtle ways.

How Conflict Escalates

To better understand how to manage and resolve conflict, you need to know what causes conflicts to escalate. Below are three common causes:

Adversarial action:

- Team members enter into *"Win-Lose Play."*
- They want to *"win"* rather than solve problems.

Tightly held positions:

- Team members see no need for achieving mutual goals.
- They harden their positions, narrow their communication, and limit involvement with one another.

Emotional involvement:

- Team members become emotionally attached to their positions.

Response To Conflict

Not everyone responds to conflict in the same way. Some natural *"reactions"* to conflict include:

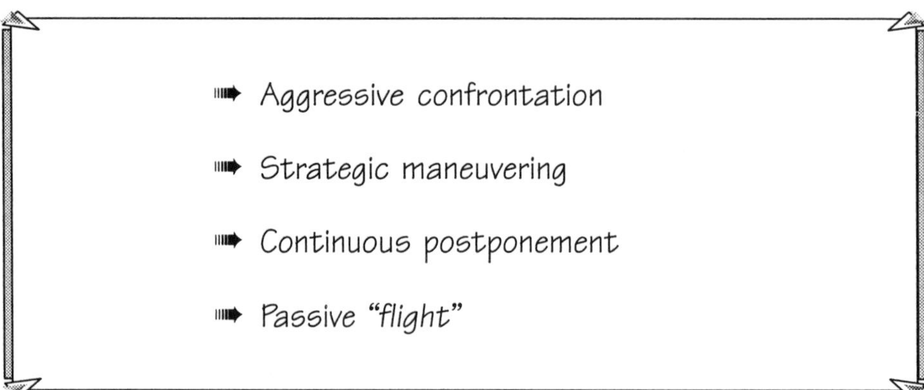

Successful *"responses"* to conflict include:

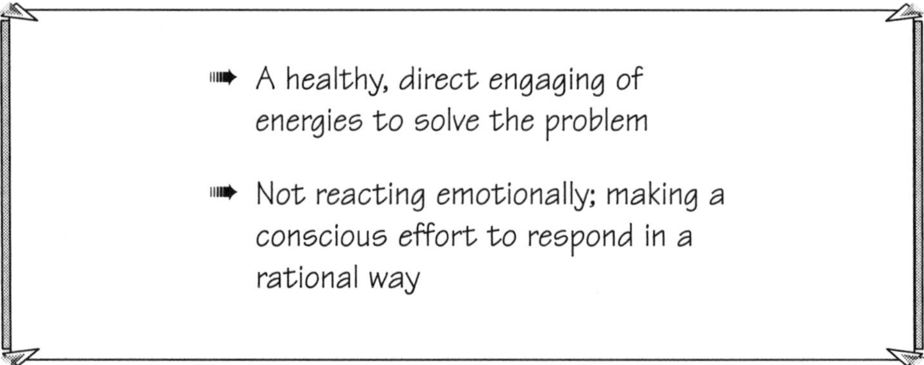

Thoughtful response to conflict strengthens teamwork and paves the way to resolving the conflict.

When Do You Act?

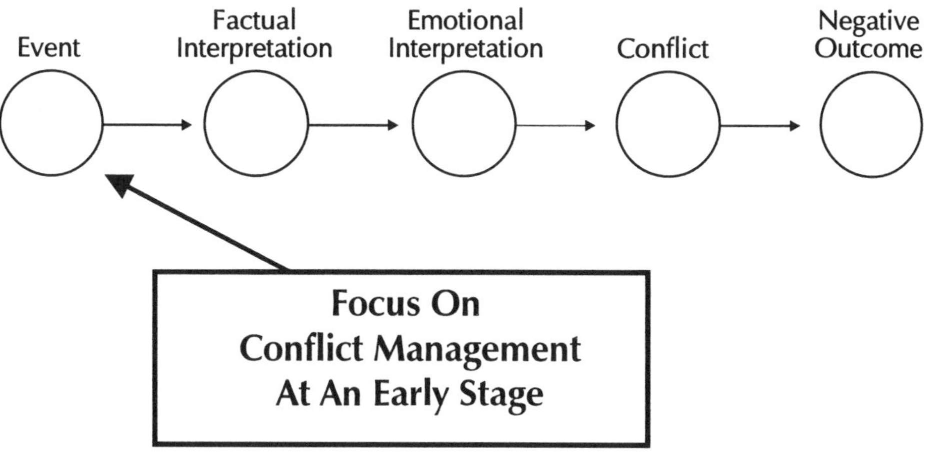

In the short run, it's easier to deny conflict than to confront it. Yet, it's easier to resolve conflict constructively when you confront it early on. At the early stage, you can focus on the factual issues of conflict before the emotional ones have had time to fester and become disruptive. Allow conflict to exist unmanaged, and you'll have a tangled web of tensions and disagreements to unravel. So catch conflict before it escalates!

Taking Steps Toward Conflict Resolution

Defusing conflict before it erupts increases your team's commitment and productivity. A dynamic team consists of a team leader and members who all take responsibility for managing conflict. That's why it's essential that all members of a team learn how to resolve conflict.

The leader may not be the first person to sense conflict. Besides, all team members should provide peer feedback, whether it consists of compliments or criticisms. Continual peer feedback helps build strong relationships and a sense of self-sufficiency.

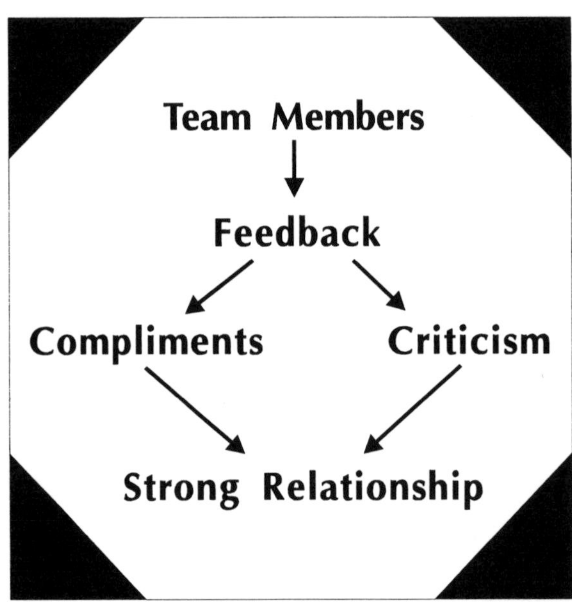

Let's take a look at a six-step conflict resolution model and how two teams used it to manage conflict.

Six Steps To Conflict Resolution

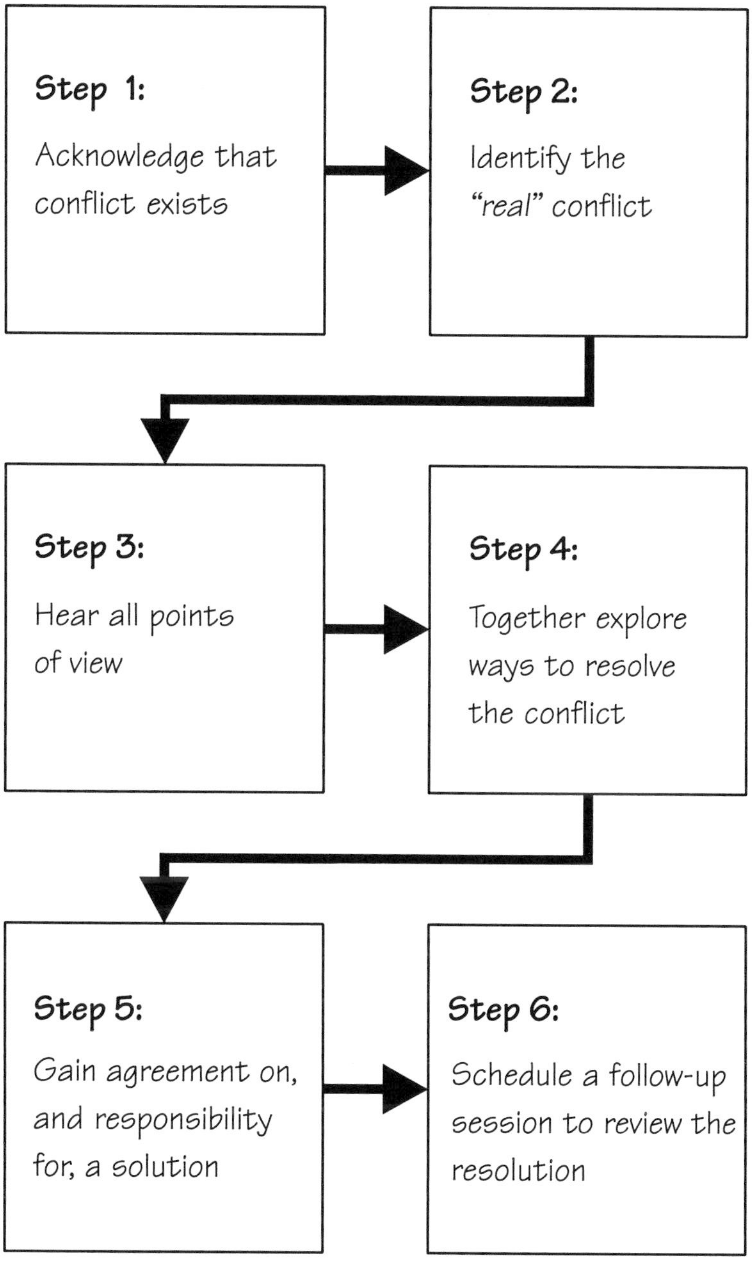

Step 1:

Acknowledge that conflict exists

Step 2:

Identify the "*real*" conflict

Step 3:

Hear all points of view

Step 4:

Together explore ways to resolve the conflict

Step 5:

Gain agreement on, and responsibility for, a solution

Step 6:

Schedule a follow-up session to review the resolution

Step 1: Acknowledge that conflict exists

If you don't address conflict immediately, it will heat up until it boils over. Then it becomes a surefire obstacle to your team's success. If you acknowledge that it exists and take steps to resolve it, you should be able to mold conflict into an opportunity.

Case Study A: ***A furniture manufacturing company . . .*** was facing a cash shortage. In response, it formed a task force to identify ways to streamline departments and save money. Mike, the team leader, asked all team members to brainstorm ways to cut costs. Robert, a new accounting supervisor, added his suggestion to the list. *"I think,"* he began,*"that cutting inventory would free up additional cash."*

"Wait just a minute," interjected Ina, a senior purchasing agent. *"You can't cut inventory. That's absolutely ludicrous." "Well, I guess we don't agree on this issue,"* Robert responded. *"Maybe we should find out why."* . . .

Case Study B: **Margaret, the leader of a team . . .**

trying to find ways to increase sales, noticed an underlying conflict between two of her team members, Reuben and Karen, both successful salespeople. Whenever Karen proposed an idea, Reuben immediately shot it down. Karen, as a result, became very quiet and withdrawn.

During one meeting, Karen recommended using telemarketing to provide additional leads for sales personnel. *"If you can't find your own leads, you don't deserve to be in sales,"* Reuben commented sarcastically. *"I don't think that was called for,"* Margaret intervened. *"We're going to stop our discussion and get to the bottom of this."*. . .

Acknowledge conflict exists

Whether you're a team member involved in a conflict *(Case Study A)*, or a team leader observing a conflict *(Case Study B)*, you must acknowledge the conflict before you can resolve it.

Step 2: Identify the "real" conflict

This step often requires diligent detective work. Identifying the real conflict is more difficult than it seems. Conflicts arise from both core issues and emotional issues.

In every conflict, there is interplay between these two kinds of issues. Even if the main conflict is about how to do something, emotional issues such as a threat to self-esteem or an outbreak of jealousy can intensify the conflict.

CORE ISSUES	EMOTIONAL ISSUES
➠ role ambiguity ➠ disagreements over methods ➠ disagreements over goals ➠ disagreements over procedures ➠ disagreements over responsibilities ➠ disagreements over values ➠ disagreements over facts	➠ incompatible personal styles ➠ struggles for control or power ➠ threats to self-esteem ➠ jealousy ➠ resentment

Core issues are most often at the base of conflict *(e.g., disagreement over tasks)*, while emotional issues complicate the conflict. For example, when one person gets a particular assignment *(core issue)* another person may become angry and feel less important *(emotional issue)*. To resolve the conflict, you must resolve the core issue first.

Case Study A: ***In Robert and Ina's case . . .***
when Robert wanted to cut inventory and Ina disagreed, the conflict was obvious. Robert thought his suggestion would help the company; Ina didn't. If Robert had not acknowledged and identified the conflict, it could have expanded.

Case Study B: ***In Reuben and Karen's case . . .***
Margaret felt that a separate meeting with just the three of them was the best way to handle the conflict. She scheduled a meeting for the next day.

In that meeting, Margaret discovered that Reuben was lashing out at Karen because she had received a transfer to a desirable sales territory that Reuben thought he should have received. His resentment of Karen's transfer was spilling over into the team meetings and stalling the team's progress. . . .

Once you've identified the real conflict, move to the next step.

Step 3: Hear all points of view

To successfully resolve conflict, you must understand both sides of the issue. Encourage team members who may be timid or unhappy to express themselves. Check for understanding and avoid debates over who is right or wrong.

In addition, discuss how the conflict is affecting people's performance. Focus on facts and behaviors, not feelings or personalities. The act of "*blaming*" causes emotions to become the center of attention.

To avoid blaming, help team members identify similarities rather than differences. Emphasizing similarities allows both sides to meet on common ground.

If differences arise, figure out the nature of the differences.

Keep in mind that:

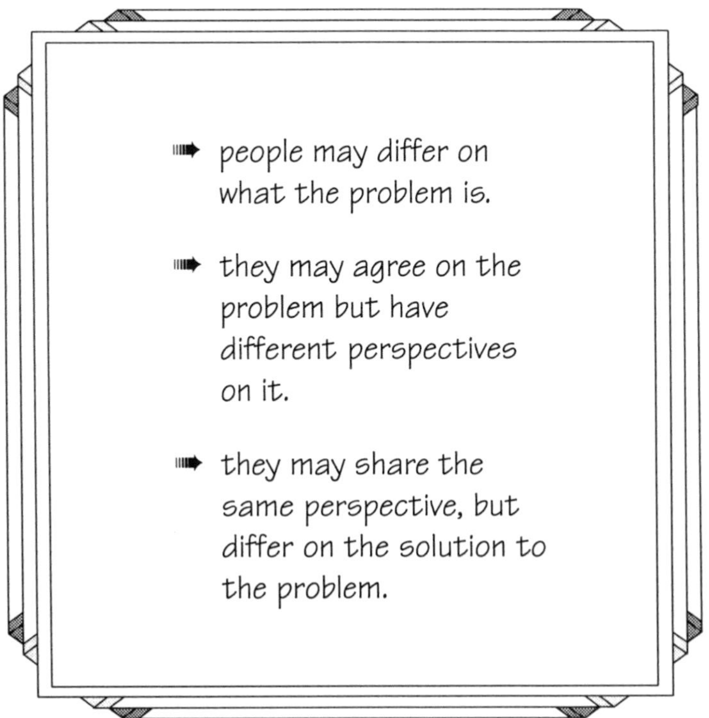

Case Study A: **At Robert's invitation . . .**

Ina opened up. *"Sure, cutting inventory will free up some extra cash,"* she said. *"But you don't have any idea what a strain it puts on us in the purchasing department."*

"You're right," Robert responded. *"I hadn't anticipated any major problems. What kind of strain would you experience?"* Ina sighed and said, *"Well, if the company receives an order from a major client and we don't have the materials in inventory, we sometimes have to buy them at a premium to meet the deadline. We don't save any money that way."*

"I'm glad you shared that point with me," Robert said. *"I think it will help all of us on the team identify a better solution."*. . .

Case Study B: **Margaret asked Reuben . . .**

to give his viewpoint and she requested that he share facts, not feelings. *"I'm not saying that Karen isn't a good salesperson,"* Reuben began, *"but I've wanted that territory for a long time, and I think management gave it to her because she's a woman." "You honestly think that's the case?"* Margaret asked. Reuben nodded. Margaret directed her gaze at Karen. *"How do you respond to that, Karen?"*

"I really feel uncomfortable with that assessment," Karen shared. *"If that were true, I'd understand Reuben's resentment. But the truth of the matter is that I've been with the company longer. Both Reuben and I are results-oriented, but I have a longer track record."*

The meeting continued, with Margaret emphasizing how their conflict affected the team. Reuben's resentment blocked his effectiveness, stifled Karen's good ideas, and hurt the team. . . .

In Robert and Ina's scenario, the two agreed on the problem; only their solutions were conflicting. Reuben and Karen had differences in perspective. Because Robert and Ina stand on common ground, their conflict should be easier to resolve.

Once all members have aired their views, it's time to come up with some ideas to resolve the conflict.

Step 4: Together explore ways to resolve the conflict

Explore each person's position, open up channels of communication, and involve others. An open discussion can result in a broadening of the information and alternatives available, and can lead to more trusting and healthy relationships between the people involved.

> **Note:** You may never get two people to like each other, but they must be able to work together!

Brainstorm ideas

Case Study A: ***Robert and Ina decided to . . .***

work toward a compromise. Robert's openness took the sting out of the conflict, making Ina more inclined to explore whether cutting inventory would hurt or help the company. Robert asked for input from the other team members, and a lively discussion ensued.

Case Study B: ***Margaret managed to . . .***

get Reuben and Karen talking to each other. She also called in the sales manager to confirm the reasoning behind Karen's transfer. The manager agreed with Karen's assessment and told Reuben that he was next in line for a transfer when a territory opened. Reuben admitted that he hadn't been fair to Karen and apologized. . . .

Now that team members have discussed ways to resolve the conflict, it's time to lock in a solution, which is exactly what the next step does.

Step 5: Gain agreement on, and responsibility for, a solution

Help members work together to solve the problem. All team members need to be as comfortable as possible with the solution. This must be a joint problem-solving session; no one should tell the other(s) how to solve the problem. You can't force agreement.

One way to help people accept one another's perspectives and joint responsibility for reaching a solution, is to have the team members do a role reversal, each person presenting another's views.

Agreement
✔ ______
✔ ______
✔ ______
✔ ______
✔ ______
✔ ______

Case Study A: ***Robert and Ina . . .***

agreed on a solution with the team's help. Ina and the purchasing department were to identify the inventory items they could cut without negative effects. For example, if a particular vendor didn't charge extra for supplying an order on short notice, stocking that item in inventory wouldn't be necessary. Ina's list would determine the extent to which the company could cut inventory. The team was satisfied with this resolution.

Case Study B: ***Margaret suggested . . .***

a role reversal for Karen and Reuben, and the results proved interesting. By putting himself in Karen's shoes, Reuben was able to acknowledge that she deserved the promotion. And Karen understood Reuben's disappointment and anger. Reuben agreed that he wouldn't thwart Karen's participation in team meetings. Karen agreed to speak up if Reuben's resentment resurfaced. . . .

And finally, let's turn to the last step in conflict resolution—evaluating its success.

Step 6: Schedule a follow-up session to review the resolution

When team members know they're going to be held accountable for carrying out a commitment, they are far more likely to honor that commitment.

Case Study A: ***Ina agreed to bring her list . . .***
of expendable inventory items to the next team meeting. The team would take a look and decide whether cutting those items would be a suggestion that they'd pass on to upper management.

Case Study B: ***Margaret asked Karen . . .***
to schedule a follow-up session after the next team meeting to review whether they had satisfactorily resolved the conflict between Karen and Reuben.

Potential Challenges

Conflict resolution is rarely easy or fast. Successful conflict resolution requires time, thought, and patience. Common barriers to conflict resolution include a team member who:

- is defensive, stubborn, and unwilling to listen.
- isn't willing to acknowledge that a conflict exists.
- is evasive and unwilling to discuss the conflict because previous attempts have been unsuccessful (i.e., he or she is too "burned-out" on the issue).
- agrees there's a conflict, but doesn't know what he or she wants.
- doesn't carry out "action items" (i.e., the team member doesn't live up to his or her side of the bargain).

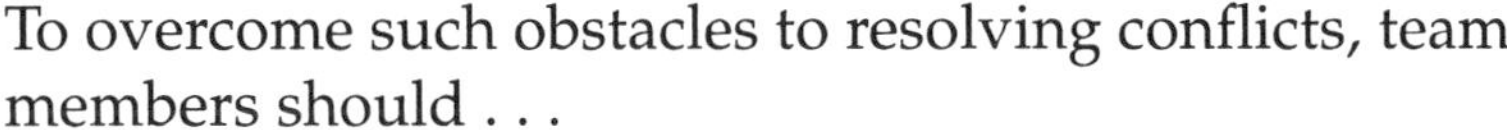

To overcome such obstacles to resolving conflicts, team members should . . .

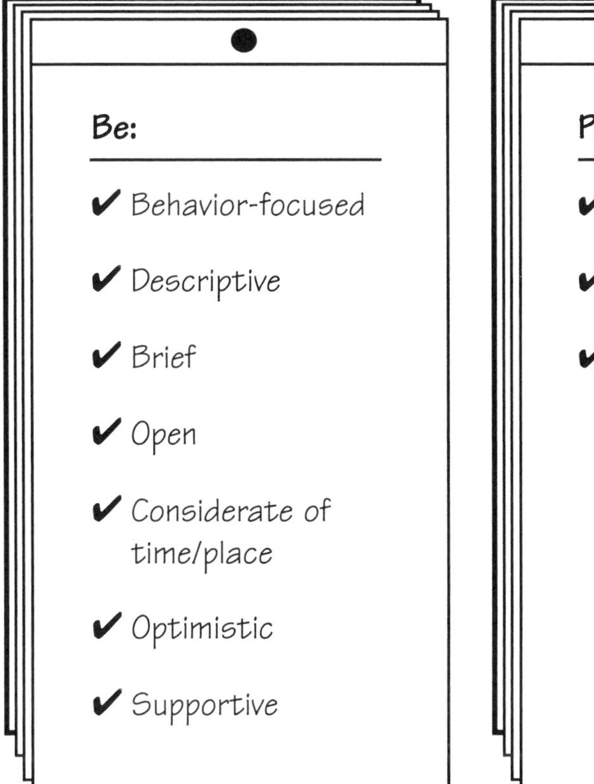

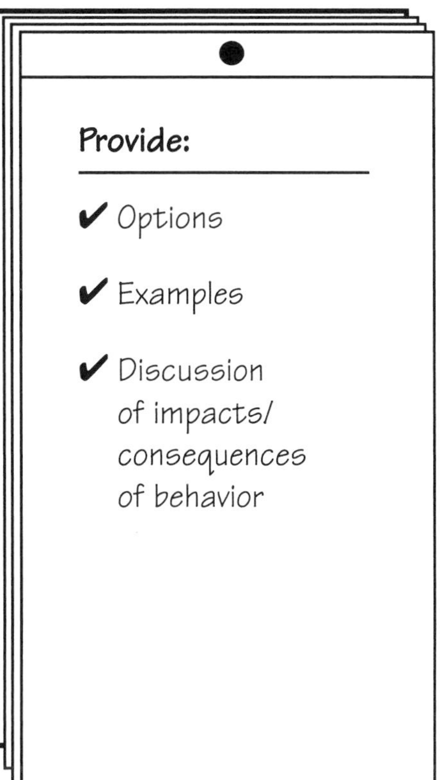

Don't rely on these behaviors only when face-to-face with conflict. Model them at every team meeting and interaction. They'll increase effective teamwork. Encouraging all team members to provide peer feedback with these behaviors in mind creates an atmosphere of productivity.

Tips For Reducing Team Conflict

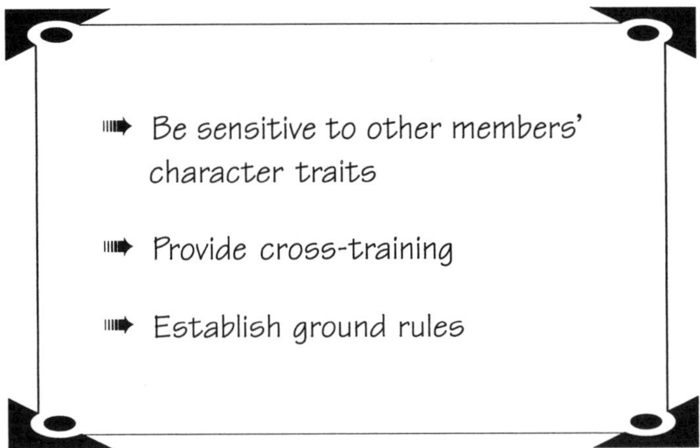

The most productive approach to dealing with conflict on teams is to take steps that actually reduce the potential for conflict before it occurs. Teams do this in a number of ways, such as sensitizing each other to their individual character traits, cross-training to learn each other's perspectives on the job at hand, and by having guidelines for team behavior, or *"ground rules."*

This last method is simple, yet very successful. If members know, understand, and agree on a set of ground rules for their team, then they will be more effective as a team.

Let's look at a combined list of the ground rules our two teams might consider to minimize the types of conflicts they had to deal with in this chapter.

Team Ground Rules

- Listen to the other team member first, then decide how to respond.
- Recognize that everyone has an opinion about almost everything.
- Acknowledge differences of opinion.
- Use the team conflict resolution model.
- Don't pass on work in a form in which you wouldn't want to receive it.
- Don't accept such work from someone else.
- When in doubt about anything, seek clarification.
- Assumptions are risky; make them only when you have to.
- Clarify where your responsibility stops and starts, and how it fits with that of other team members.
- Update people who need to know what you know.
- If you have an issue or point of disagreement with a team member, tell them, not others.

Chapter Five Worksheet: Fielding Conflicting Messages

1. Examine the following two critical remarks and develop an appropriate response to each.

a) You usually do an excellent job, but lately you've been careless, sometimes making obvious mistakes. A team member criticizes you, *"You constantly make mistakes on these reports. I just can't believe it! I thought you knew your job. Why can't you be more careful?"*

b) You are attending an important meeting. You want to get the group to adopt your ideas without turning off the members who have stated strong opposing opinions. The team leader thinks your ideas are poor and interrupts your presentation, showing little respect, *"You can't be serious about this proposal. It's just like three past efforts that fell far short of their goals. Just listen to me now . . ."*

2. What ground rules can you set up to help minimize conflict within your team?

ACCEPTING TEAM DIVERSITY

Everybody on your team cannot possibly be exactly like you. The other members don't think the same way or hold the same values as you. And while a team of clones might be conflict-free, it would lack the diversity that stimulates new ideas.

However, a team of diverse individuals has challenges. Differences in personality, culture, gender, goals, sexual preferences, etc., can present difficulties. Unless your team exhibits trust, respect, and openness, it will be wracked with conflict or stifled into uselessness.

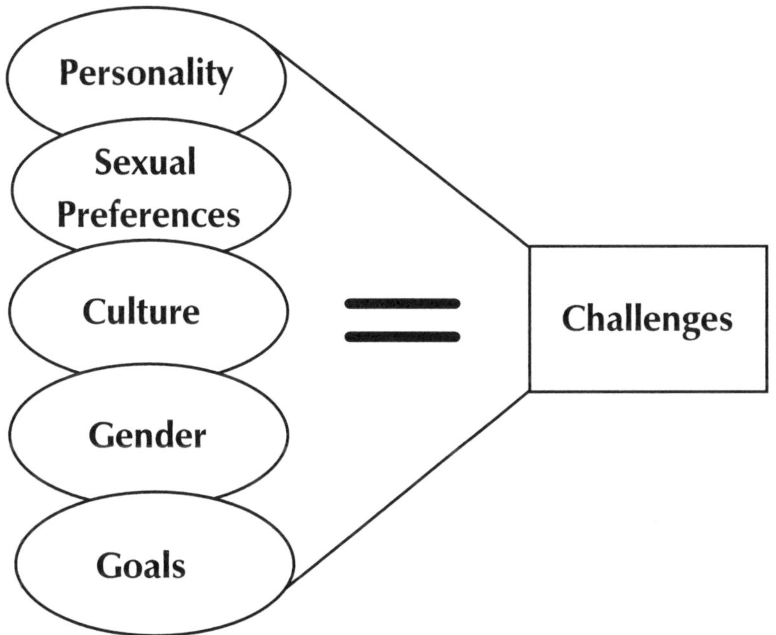

Characteristics Of Dynamic And Diverse Teams

Following are three characteristics of teams that are committed to working together. A team that models these accepts all members and uses their strengths for the benefit of the team.

Opinion-oriented

- ✔ The opposite of opinionated, this characteristic steers members away from condemning others.
- ✔ Opinion-oriented members introduce their ideas without suggesting or even hinting that others need to alter theirs.
- ✔ Team members state their opinions and ask for others' opinions, instead of asserting that they have *"the answer."*
- ✔ They don't focus solely on their own ideas; they investigate the ideas of others.

Equality-minded

- ✔ In any diverse group, being equality-minded is a prerequisite for effective communication.
- ✔ Equality-minded team members see diversity as an advantage: *"Our differing views allow us to check out every side, corner, top, and bottom of an issue."*
- ✔ A team that is equality-minded relies on its members.
- ✔ Reliance on team members increases productivity.

Goal-focused

- ✔ Team members who focus on the goals of the group are less likely to quibble about uniquenesses.
- ✔ The entire team has a similar purpose.
- ✔ To goal-focused members, uniquenesses are not issues.
- ✔ Team members recognize that individuals have goals too, and these can come into conflict with team goals.
- ✔ Members' uniquenesses are brought to the surface and dealt with, not left to cause problems down the road.

A team that exhibits these characteristics builds an atmosphere of trust and caring. The team members have attitudes that serve as an open channel for communication. If every team modeled these characteristics, diversity wouldn't be an issue. In the real world, though, communication often breaks down when people don't understand or accept uniquenesses.

Take a look at these two scenarios, in which uniquenesses challenge a team's performance:

Case Study C: **Dave, a team leader . . .**
sees Annalisa, a new employee whose knowledge of English is limited, and member of his team, completing a new process of logging in data. The team is evaluating this process. Dave asks Annalisa to fill out an evaluation form on the process and bring it to the next meeting. *"Will you do that for me?"* he asks. She responds, *"Yes."* The next day when Dave asks for the evaluation form, Annalisa is empty-handed. Dave's not thrilled.

Case Study D: **Chad and Vicki . . .**
fellow team members, are working together on annual budget reports. Chad laughs. *"Okay,"* he says, *"but I might as well do it myself. A man can accomplish a lot more than a woman can."* Vicki's blood starts boiling. Chad has never worked with her on an assignment before. . . .

Understanding Frames Of Reference

To understand the actions and attitudes of others who have frames of reference different from your own, carefully focus on the following two major processes.

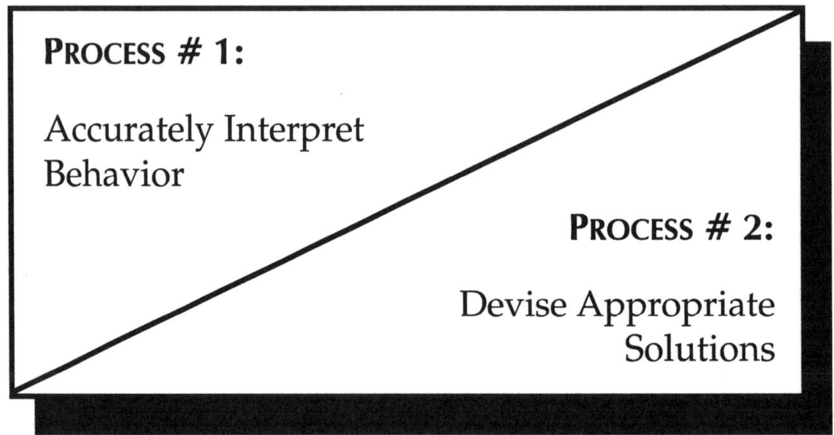

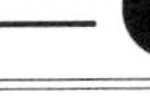

Process # 1: Accurately interpret behavior

Strive to accurately interpret the behavior of the team member who thinks or acts differently than you do. This process consists of three key steps:

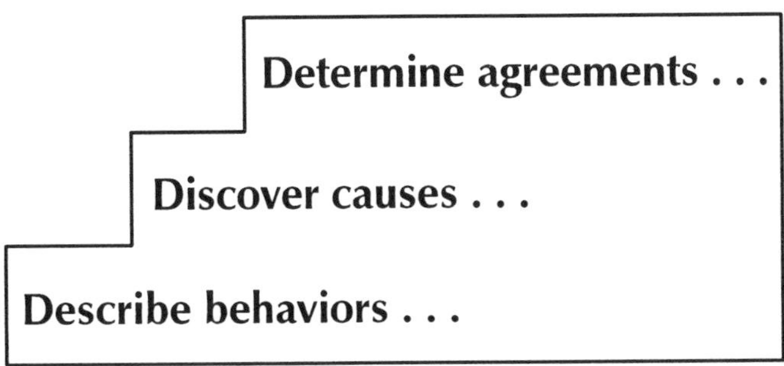

Step 1: Describe, don't evaluate, your behavior and the behavior of your team member

Describing the behaviors of both members eliminates emotional undertones. The goal is to look at the situation objectively.

Here's an objective description of what took place in our two scenarios:

Case Study C: ***Dave asks . . .***

Annalisa to complete an evaluation form and bring it to the next meeting. Annalisa agrees, but doesn't complete the task.

Case Study D: ***Chad agrees . . .***

to work on an assigned project with Vicki, but believes and implies that she won't contribute equally since she's a woman. . . .

Step 2: Discover the underlying causes of each member's behavior

Why do you think the other team member behaved in the way you described in Step 1? If you can identify the underlying causes, it will be easier to solve the problem.

Underlying Causes

Underlying Causes

Underlying Causes

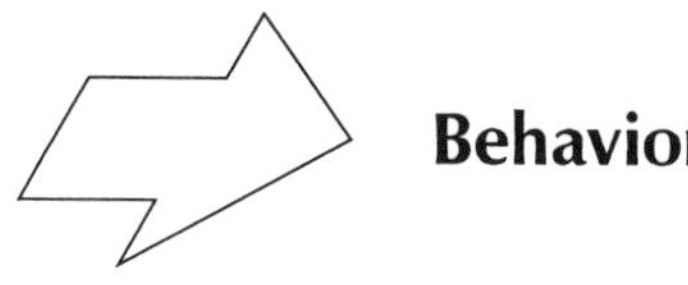

Behavior

Case Study C: ***To Dave, an affirmative response . . .***
translates into acceptance of his request. For Annalisa, it is difficult to say no to an elder, particularly a male leader. Her response may have simply meant that she heard what he said, not that she understood how to complete the task.

Case Study D: ***From Chad's point of view, . . .***
men can complete tasks faster and better than women. To Vicki, such a statement is an unacceptable stereotype. . . .

Step 3: Determine areas of agreement, and put yourself in your team member's shoes

Look for the similarities between you and the other team member. Try to understand the uniquenesses by putting yourself in your team member's place.

Behavior of the Team

Effective Solutions

Case Study C: ***Both Dave and Annalisa . . .***
want the task done correctly. If Dave had to fill out an unfamiliar form in a language other than his native one, he, too, might have difficulty.

Case Study D: ***Both Chad and Vicki want . . .***
to do their assignment correctly and on time. Neither knows how competent the other is. If the situations were reversed and Vicki made a comment similar to Chad's, Chad, too, might have found it demeaning. . . .

Once you've accurately interpreted the behavior of the team members involved, begin the second process—working toward an effective solution.

Process # 2: Devise appropriate solutions

This allows you to use the information and ideas generated in the first process to help you resolve uniquenesses. Devising appropriate solutions also consists of three key steps.

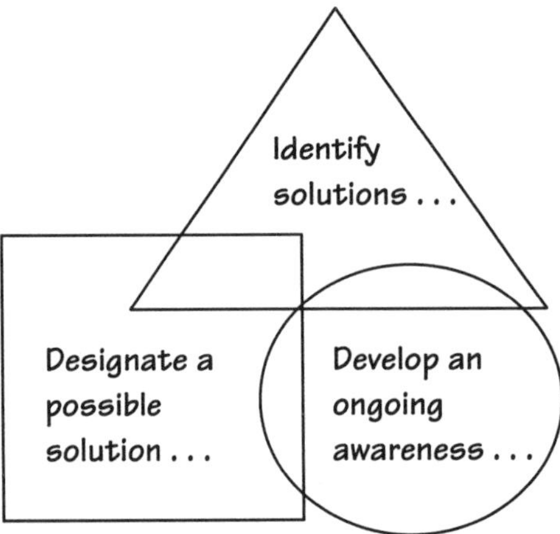

Step 1: Identify solutions based on input about uniquenesses among team members

General solutions won't work. The difficulty exists because of uniquenesses. You must factor these uniquenesses into the solution to achieve your goal of increasing effective teamwork.

Case Study C: ***Dave came up with three . . .***

solutions. First, he could show Annalisa how to fill out the evaluation form and ask her to paraphrase what he does at each step.

Secondly, Dave knows that Binh, another team member, understands how to complete the form. He could ask Binh to show Annalisa how to fill out the form. He could also ask Binh to choose two members of the team *(one of whom would be Annalisa)* to discuss this task with all members of the team, thus *"quality checking"* the group.

Lastly, during a team meeting, he could demonstrate the task and ask members to check one another's forms at the next meeting.

Case Study D: ***Vicki came up with two . . .***

possible solutions. First, she could talk with Chad privately and discuss how his stereotypical remark affected her. Or secondly, she could work with Chad on the reports and prove to him that his perception was unfounded. . . .

Step 2: Designate a possible solution, act on it, and then evaluate its success

This is the implementation stage. Decide which of your solutions will be most effective and put it into practice. Finally, determine if it was successful.

Case Study C: ***Dave decided to implement the solution . . .*** involving Binh because it used peer group support from other team members. The next day, Dave received a form that Annalisa had filled out. It was complete and correct. The solution was a success.

Case Study D: ***Vicki chose to combine her two solutions . . .*** proving her competence first, then talking with Chad. The talk seemed to help. Chad admitted that he had misjudged Vicki. He had been worried that she might dump the assignment on him, and he didn't realize that she'd take his remark personally. *"Very few women wouldn't take it personally,"* Vicki responded. Chad promised to curb his comments.

At the next meeting, Chad apologized to the team for his comment and praised Vicki's work. *"Vicki did a great job on the reports,"* he said. *"In fact, she probably contributed more than I did."* Vicki felt her solution was successful. . . .

On to the final step which helps lay the groundwork for minimizing future problems related to team member diversity.

Step 3: Develop an ongoing awareness of the challenges of diversity and the need to meet those challenges successfully

Here's the hard part! While one successful solution is certainly cause for celebration, the challenges of diversity are ongoing. If your team members remain aware of them, diversity can be one of your team's best advantages.

Here's how the people in our two scenarios can meet ongoing diversity challenges:

Case Study C: ***Dave might consider continuing . . .***
to use quality checks for different tasks, thus improving performance while accepting that different team members learn in different ways.

Case Study D: ***In Vicki and Chad's team . . .***
continual discussion of attitudes could be helpful. Constant reinforcement of each member's value to the team could also keep morale high.

How team members understand and work with individual uniquenesses directly affects a team's performance. The examples in this chapter do not include all the uniquenesses that could show up in a team. And don't disregard this chapter just because, for example, your team consists of 10 white males between the ages of 35 and 40. Personalities and attitudes can be the most divisive uniquenesses of all.

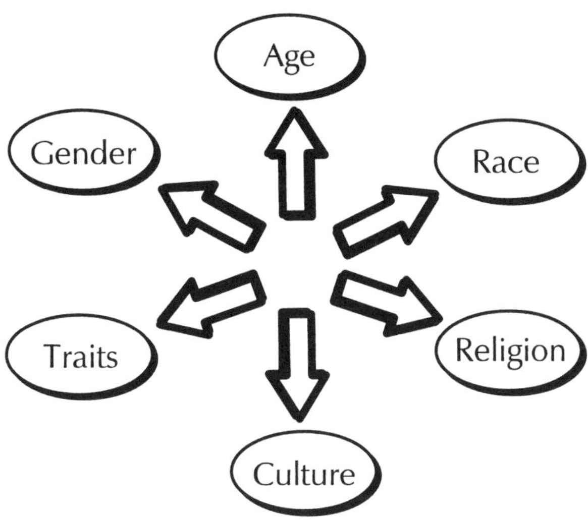

All types of uniquenesses can push a team toward its goals. For example, a quiet team member can be just as productive as an assertive member. You may assume that the less assertive team member doesn't have good ideas to contribute, while in fact he or she is processing information carefully and may have great ideas if given the chance to share them.

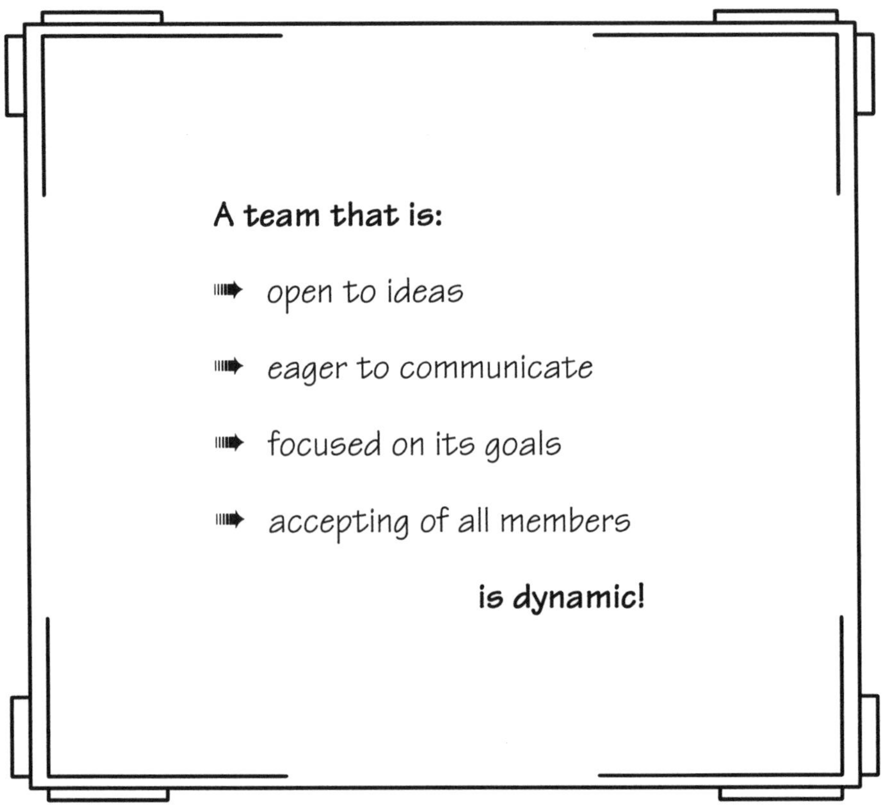

Remember, team diversity isn't an option; using it to your advantage is!

Chapter Six Worksheet: Accepting Individual Members

1. List some of the uniquenesses among the members of your team.

2. How would you rate your team in terms of the behavior models that encourage communication? Rate yourself individually and then rate your team on a scale of 1 to 10, with 10 meaning the model describes you and/or your team exactly.

	You	Your team
a) Opinion-oriented:	____________	____________
b) Equality-minded:	____________	____________
c) Goal-focused:	____________	____________

Comments:

____

____

____

____

____

____

____

____

3. Choose two *"unique"* behaviors related to diversity that you've observed in your team, and explain the reasons *(rationale)* for your choices. Base your choices on the frequency with which you observe the behaviors, how severely they impact your team, or other criteria.

Choice # 1 and Rationale:

____

____

____

____

____

____

____

Choice # 2 and Rationale:

____

____

____

____

____

____

____

Motivating Your Team

Any book on improving teamwork would be incomplete without a chapter on motivation. Why? Because motivation stimulates members to excel and pushes the team forward to meet its goals. Motivate your team, and you'll reach your goals in less time and with more satisfaction.

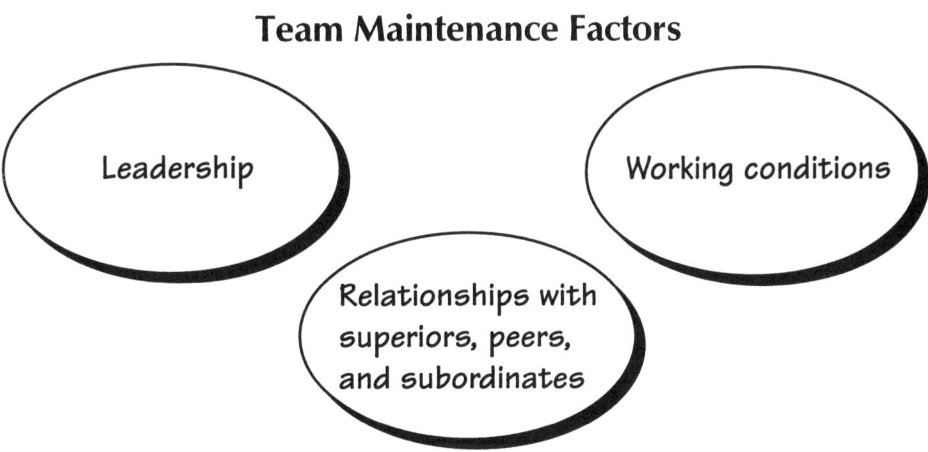

Consider Maintenance Factors

Before you tackle motivation, though, consider some factors that do not motivate by themselves, but are necessary to keep your team from experiencing dissatisfaction. These are basic to productive teamwork. Following are some of the maintenance factors you can control.

Leadership

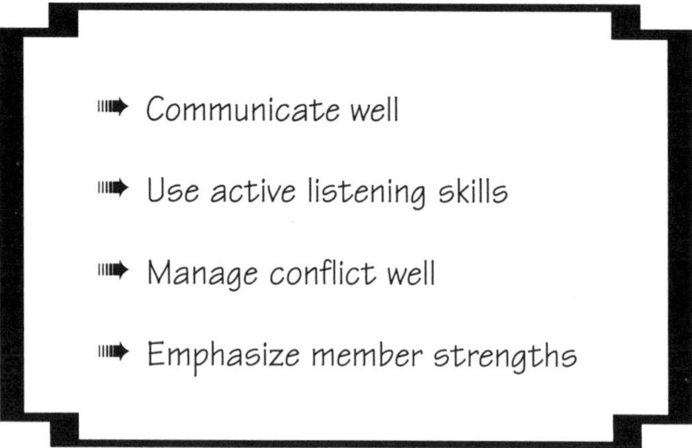

The previous chapters covered ways to improve communication and relationships within your team. If you are a team leader, or are the temporary leader of a team project, your handling of communication is a key part of your job.

If you're on top of communication, use active listening skills, manage conflict well, and emphasize the strengths of your diverse team members, your team will be satisfied with your team leadership.

Working Conditions

The other factor that you can control is working conditions. Are you meeting at the end of the day when your team members are tired and yearning to go home? Try meeting at a more productive time. Are you meeting during the lunch hour? Reschedule the meeting or provide lunch.

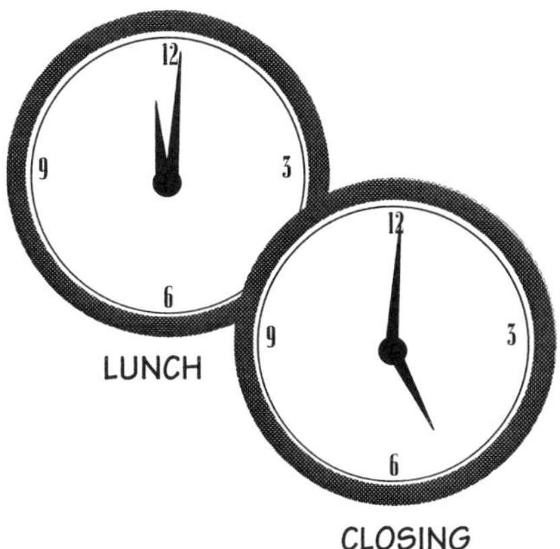

Where are you meeting? Is there enough room, or do you have to rub elbows? Consider lighting, temperature, and any other factors that affect productivity. Think about the length of your meetings and the time between them. Are you providing enough time to cover all you want to accomplish? Have you scheduled so many meetings that your team members dread attending another one?

Don't neglect maintenance factors. While they don't motivate, they go a long way toward reducing dissatisfaction. If you're in tune with your team on these issues, you're providing an atmosphere that lends itself to motivation.

Use Motivating Factors

Motivating factors relate to the nature and content of the work your team members are performing. When these factors are present, they build high levels of motivation. The motivators that encourage teams to excel include:

If these factors are not present, it doesn't mean that dissatisfaction sets in. As long as you consider the maintenance factors, you can have a satisfied team that communicates and accomplishes work. You can even have a partially effective team. But motivating factors provide additional power. They can help you reach goals faster, come up with additional ideas, and increase work performance.

Motivate Committed Team Members

As the team leader or a team member who is trying to motivate others, determine what motivates the person you want to motivate. You won't motivate a team member with a challenging project if challenging work in and of itself doesn't motivate him or her. Perhaps the possibility of a promotion is a motivator. If so, you can motivate that team member by noting that the project may help him or her get a promotion.

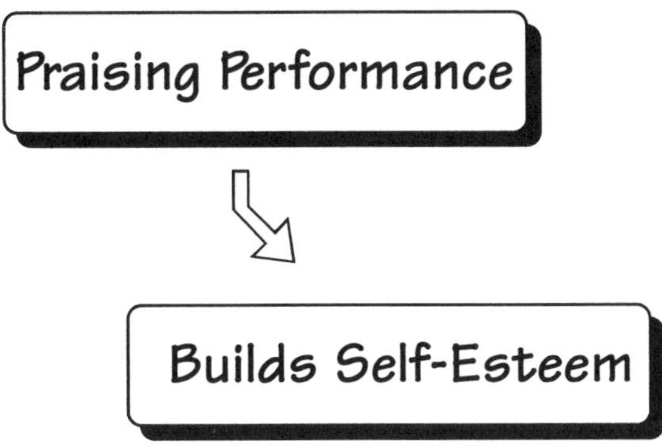

For another member, the motivator may be increased responsibility. He or she is motivated to master new skills and become more valuable to the organization. For someone else, success may be a key motivator. That team member's productivity increases when he or she completes a task successfully. That person is then ready for a new assignment that again allows him or her to demonstrate his or her ability to achieve.

Nearly everyone appreciates recognition for a job well done. A good team leader recognizes every person who contributes to the team. Different people may prefer different rewards, but all enjoy recognition and rewards for tasks they have successfully completed. Refer to the *"Motivational Options"* table in the Appendix, which suggests a number of recognitions and rewards that you can use.

You may have to make some hit-and-miss attempts before you determine how to motivate some members of your team. The challenge is that what motivates a person one day might not work six months later. Don't give up. Motivation isn't something you can ignore just because it's not an exact science. Work at it and your team will benefit.

Motivate Unmotivated Team Members

Not all team members are equally motivated to participate and be productive. In addition to motivating productive members, you must motivate average or nonparticipating members to increase their commitment to the team.

The following strategies can help you turn nonparticipating team members into active participants:

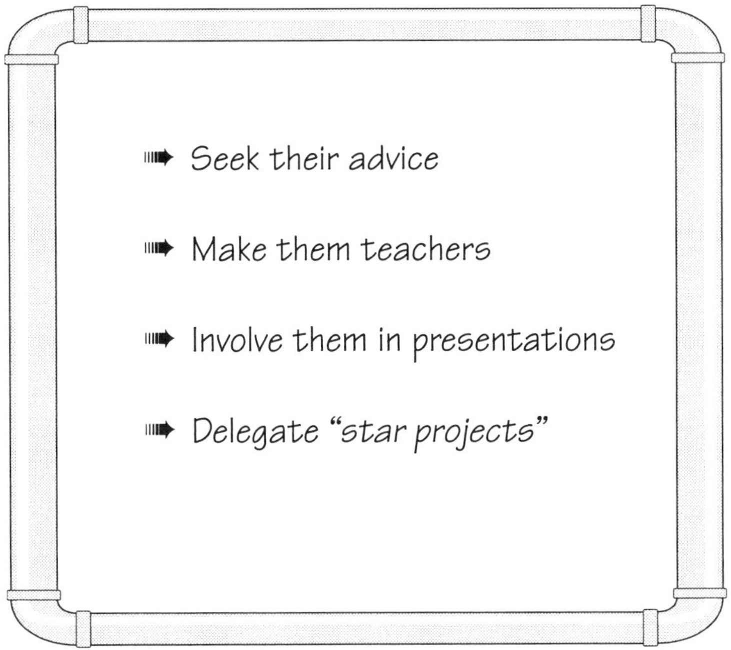

Seek their advice

By asking for the advice of a nonparticipating team member, you show that you value his or her expertise.

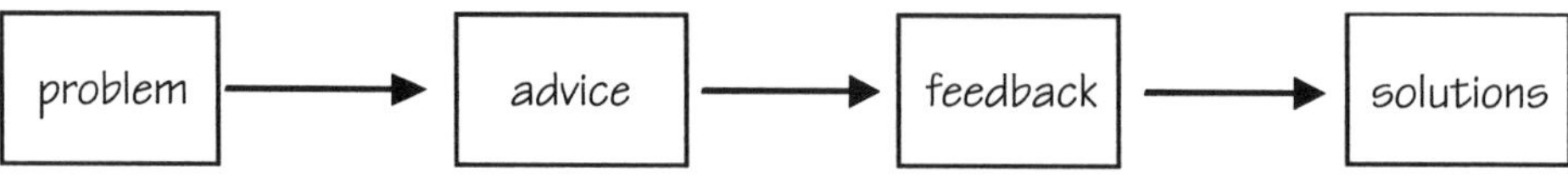

Don, a longtime employee . . .

and a member of a newly formed team, rarely contributed to team discussions. Janice, the team leader, asked for his advice on an issue about which he was knowledgeable. Don responded, and the positive feedback he received from Janice and other members motivated him to take a more active role.

Don later confided, *"I didn't want to be on the team. I thought they were a bunch of young upstarts with a lot of the same ideas I'd heard before. Ideas that didn't work then and wouldn't work now. But when I realized that they really wanted to improve our organization and were willing to listen to what I'd learned from experience, I changed my mind."...*

It's critical that your team members feel they are contributing to the success of the team and your organization. Encourage their suggestions and provide feedback. Ignoring or forgetting their suggestions is worse than not asking for them in the first place!

Make them teachers

Most nonparticipating team members become more active when you assign them a role. Identify a necessary task that the team member can do well, then ask that person to teach a less-experienced team member the task. Emphasize that the assignment is important, so that the team member knows he or she is making a significant contribution.

Rhonda, a member of a team . . .

that had been meeting for six months, was no longer participating. Her mind was always elsewhere, especially when Jim, the team leader, asked for her suggestions. Jim approached her after one meeting and asked her to take Krista under her wing. *"Krista needs some help understanding our new computer procedure. She's having problems that are affecting her performance and self-esteem. You know the procedure very well. Would you meet with her over the next week and make sure she has a handle on it?"* Rhonda agreed, and the next week she participated in the team meeting, giving some input on the new procedure. . . .

Involve them in presentations

Sometimes a nonparticipating team member feels that his or her contributions aren't necessary. If the team member can handle it, ask him or her to present ideas, plans, or findings to your team or even to upper management or other departments. You can ask a less assertive or less knowledgeable team member to help you set up flip charts or record brainstorming ideas. Directed involvement often translates into voluntary involvement.

Allen, a team leader . . .

used this method to motivate two of his team members. Both were not participating actively on the team, but for different reasons. Sally, a high-energy employee, felt the team was a waste of time. Ben was shy. Allen asked Sally to present some of the team's findings to the president of the company. This showed Sally that the team was important, and she returned with new enthusiasm. Allen directed Ben to list ideas on a flip chart in front of the team. This gave Ben confidence, and he became more willing to speak up in discussions. . . .

Delegate "star projects"

This is similar to the previous example in which you involve a team member in giving a presentation. In this instance, you choose a competent team member and assign him or her a special job. You're giving the member an opportunity to shine. If the special job involves other members, put your chosen team member in charge. You'll be able to observe his or her leadership and organizational abilities, and that team member will be challenged.

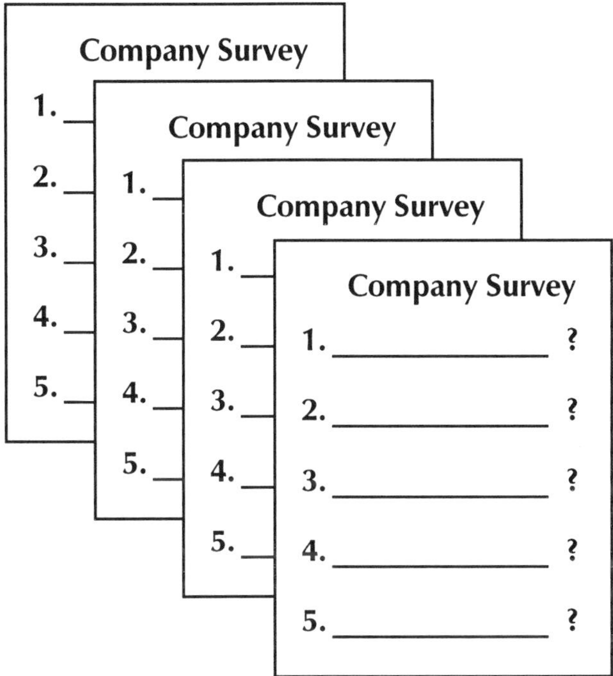

Jherri, a loner in one group . . .

undertook a special company-wide survey. With the help of two other team members, she completed the task and presented their findings to the team. Less than a month went by before Jherri volunteered to head another project.

If none of these methods motivates your nonparticipating team members, you can simply tolerate these members, hope they change on their own, or transfer them out of your team. Another possibility is to talk with them individually outside the team meetings. Use your active listening skills. It's possible that personal problems are affecting their performance. If so, time may be the best solution.

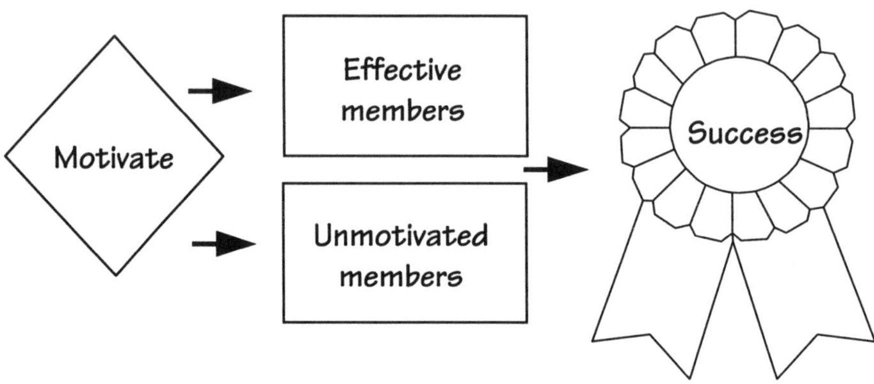

Motivating both effective participants and nonparticipating members is a key to unlocking your team's potential for success.

Chapter Seven Worksheet: Motivating For Productivity

1. List the *"maintenance"* factors that are present in your team meetings. Are they keeping your team from feeling dissatisfied?

2. List the members in your team who are not participating as actively as they should.

3. Choose one nonparticipating team member and describe how you could use the four strategies to motivate him or her.

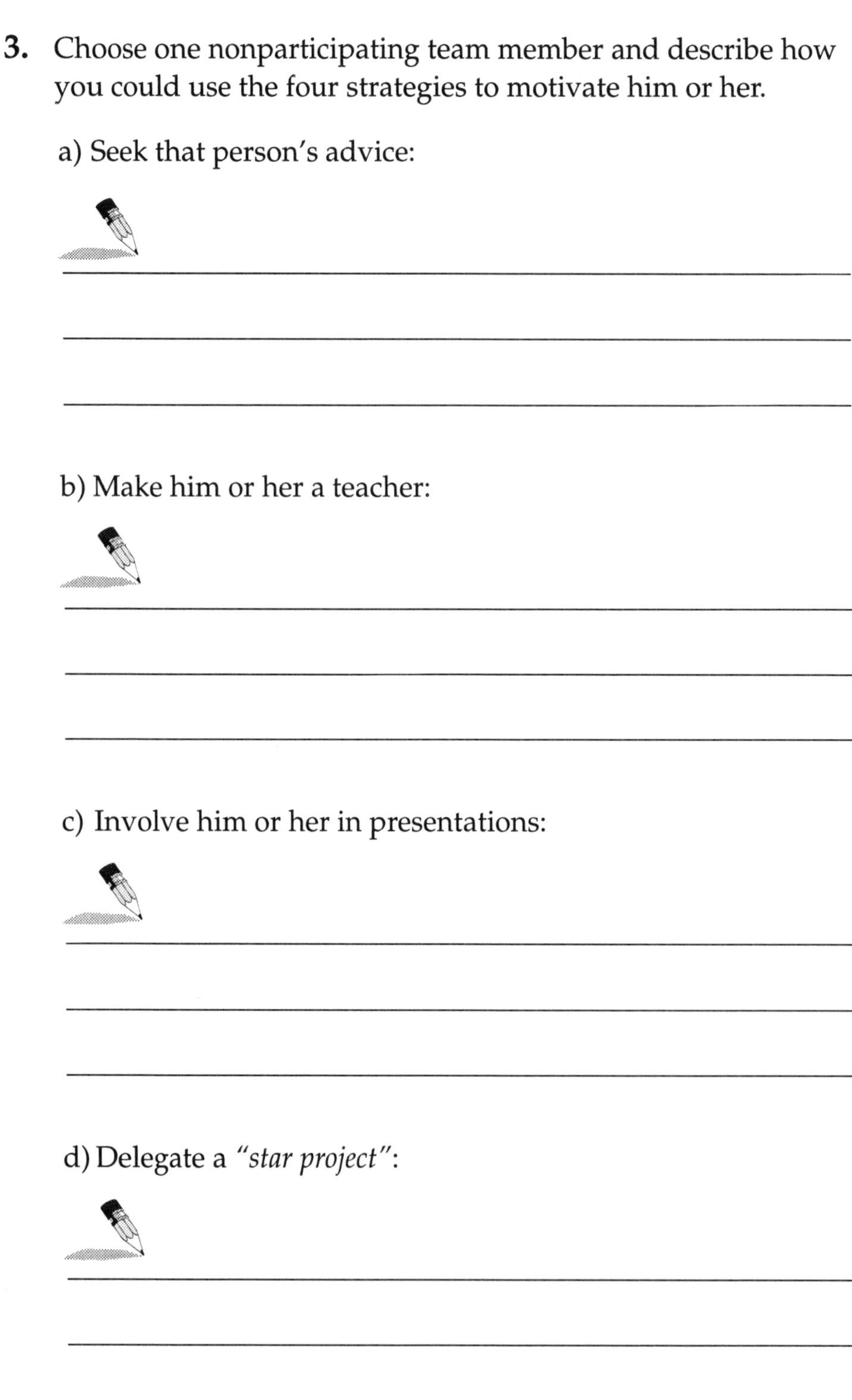

a) Seek that person's advice:

b) Make him or her a teacher:

c) Involve him or her in presentations:

d) Delegate a *"star project"*:

4. On the *"Motivational Options"* page in the Appendix, check the rewards and recognition you could use to increase your team members' productivity. Please describe how you would do this.

CHAPTER EIGHT

Summary

You're ready! You've worked through this guidebook and learned how to change your team from dull to dynamic. Time to begin.

☑ You've read about ideas to improve communication among team members, including possible barriers to, and enhancers of, effective communication. Communication lies at the heart of team dynamics, and is often the root cause of all types of issues that come up in teams. Use the tips and techniques presented here with your team members.

☑ Active listening means just what it says—team members need to focus on taking active roles as listeners. This concept is very straightforward on paper. The only way to make it work, though, is for team members to make a point of practicing it on an ongoing basis.

☑ Conflicts are inevitable. Teams can go a long way toward managing conflict by taking steps to minimize its occurrence. If team members have a consistent approach, or model for dealing with it, conflict can be used as a cue for new ideas, or to bring problems to the surface. Make sure your team does both.

☑ Team members with diverse backgrounds bring new and valuable perspectives to the table. Recognize, however, that these perspectives might differ widely from one member to another. Ensure that your team recognizes these unique perspectives, values, and ideas as potential contributors to the team's success.

☑ Motivation is often described as something that is generated internally. It is the responsibility of individuals on a team to be self-motivated. You have read about techniques the team can use to create the environment for this to come true, and to maintain team member motivation.

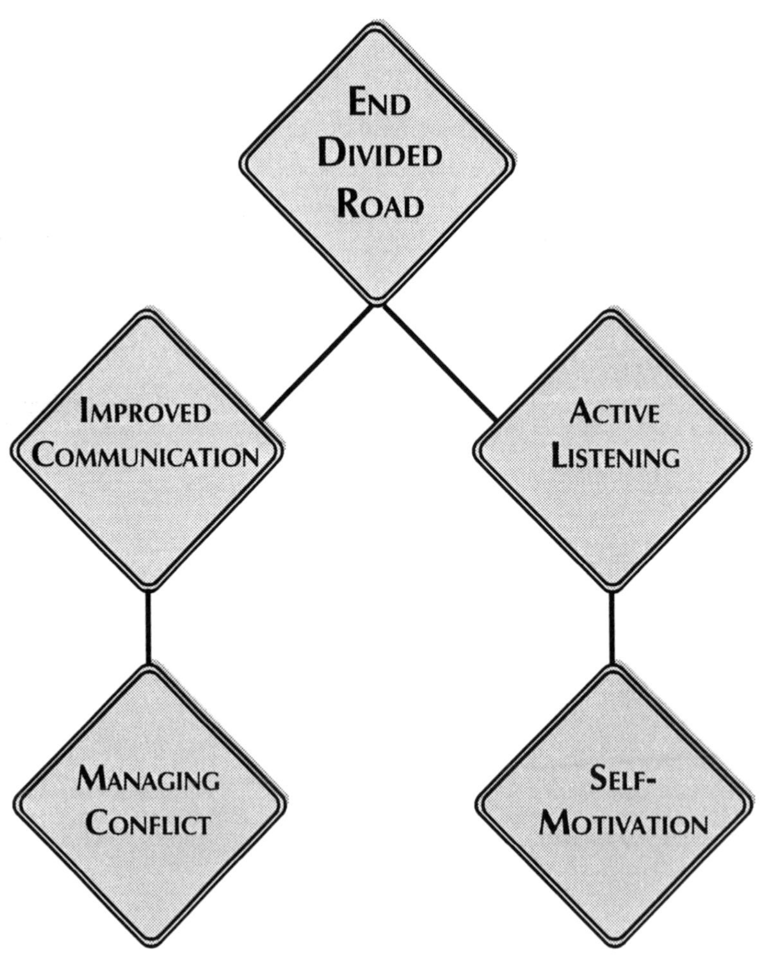